W9-AHC-432

SPLENDID LOW-CARB DESSERTS

A Splendid Guide for Creating Low-Carb Desserts
By Jennifer Eloff

Author of National Best-selling Cookbooks

*Splendid Low-Carbing, More Splendid Low-Carbing
And Splendid Low-Carbing for Life (vol-1)
Splendid Desserts* and *More Splendid Desserts*

Canadian Cataloguing in Publication Data
Eloff, Jennifer, 1957
Splendid Low-Carb Desserts
First Printing ~ April 2004

ISBN 0-7795-0067-9   Includes Index.
1. Low-carb diet recipes. 2. Sugarless recipes.
3. Desserts, low-carb recipes.
4.   Title 5. A Splendid Guide for Creating Low-Carb Desserts.

Inspiration: Thank you God from the bottom of my heart!
Photography: Ian Eloff and Ross Hutchinson
Front and Back Cover Design: Ian and Jonathan Eloff
Web-site Enhancements: Daniel and Ian Eloff
Printed in Calgary, Canada by **Blitzprint** (www.Blitzprint.com)

Pictured on front cover: Lime Cheesecake, Blueberry Swirl Cheesecake &
Raspberry Lemon Cheesecake
Pictured on back cover: Chocolate Sweetheart Cake, Golden Fruitcake, Vanilla
Cheesecake, The Best
Brownies, Classic Peanut Butter Cookies, Pecan
Chocolate Sweetheart Cake, Pumpkin Chip Muffins

Published by **Eureka Publishing**

CONTENTS

INTRODUCTION

All recipes are below 10 grams carbohydrate per serving and many are significantly less. Desserts are often by their very nature carbohydrate-filled, therefore, to make delicious, creative low-carb desserts that resemble their high-carb counterparts has become a bit of an art form in the low-carb world. Some people think it is simply not possible to duplicate high-carb desserts with great success, however, it is my hope that this book will change minds about that. I believe it really is possible for low-carbers to have their cake and eat it too!!!

Creating tasty, low-carb desserts has been a learning curve for me. This book contains some real breakthroughs, not the least of which is the Low-Carb Bake Mix, page 22 and Vital Oat Ultimate Bake Mix, page 20, which has enabled me to convert many high-carb desserts with ease. Now you can do the same with your own recipes.

You will notice there are several confections. Often the sweet treat is not for company, but for us, to keep cravings for sugary treats at bay and to feel satisfied with our food on a daily basis. We do not need to feel deprived.

Desserts are one of the comfort foods in life and if you have a sweet tooth like mine, you will understand what I'm saying. The question is can one regularly have desserts and other legal treats, while trying to lose weight on a low-carb diet? The answer is really dependent on the individual. We are all different. My opinion is that it is possible; however, if you are going to have something sweet every day, make it after your main meal of the day and not something you snack on during the rest of the day. This will avoid insulin spikes. For others, something sweet in the house will call their name constantly, and for those folks, desserts will need to be an occasional indulgence. We all need a special treat sometimes, be it on weekends, be it on a special occasion like a birthday or a dinner party with friends. At restaurants, I have been known to quietly bring out my cheesecake or other dessert at the end of a meal to have along with my tea. I have never been thrown out of a restaurant or even scolded. I simply explain if the waitress or waiter inquires, that it is a sugarless, low-carb dessert. Typically, there is no such thing on the menu, but this is bound to change.

After a light meal, it makes sense that a richer, more elaborate dessert would not be out of place and visa versa. Entertaining the low-carb way can now be done in style and without embarrassment of serving a dessert afterwards that is substandard. The higher fat content combined with the techniques shown in this cookbook makes for luxurious desserts that your company will no doubt enjoy and marvel at since they are sugarless, low-carb and often flourless. Look for many beautiful photos of desserts, etc. from all the cookbooks on our websites.

HELPFUL HINTS

1. ***Usable Carbs or Net Carbs*** = carbohydrates per serving minus the fiber. The reason for this is that the value for the carbohydrates calculated is actually the carbohydrates plus the fiber. Most fiber is indigestible or poorly absorbed. The carbohydrate values shown in all the recipes and their variations are actually the usable carbs (carbs minus fiber), so the math has already been done for you. ***Optional ingredients*** are not included in the nutritional analysis.

2. Unless otherwise specified, large ***eggs*** are used. Light-tasting (also light in color) ***olive oil*** is used to impart negligible flavor to desserts. ***Dutch cocoa*** is a milder-tasting cocoa and preferable in these recipes.

3. ***Da Vinci® Gourmet Sugar Free Syrups*** were used for flavor, sweetness and to reduce carbs in many recipes, however, I always endeavored to give alternatives wherever possible.

4 ***SPLENDA® Granular*** is not as effective at sweetening cocoa and unsweetened baking chocolate recipes as sugar, fructose and other sweeteners such as sugar alcohols. The SPLENDA® packets will do a better job of sweetening cocoa and baking chocolate recipes, but in baking with chocolate it is best to use the packets in combination with SPLENDA® Granular. This is not the case in confections, frostings, cheesecakes, ice creams, popsicles and some puddings, etc., where either version of the sweetener will work. In fact, if you notice an aftertaste in some of my chocolate confections (I don't notice it, although my younger son claims to detect an aftertaste sometimes), then use the SPLENDA® packets, as this seems to solve the problem for Jonathan. (24 packets = 1 cup SPLENDA® Granular, although sometimes one can use far fewer packets (maybe only 8 to 12, thereby reducing carbs) as they are sweeter than SPLENDA® Granular.)

5. Some desserts use ***sugarless chocolate chips*** (usually sweetened with maltitol, a sugar alcohol). It is clear that some people cannot tolerate maltitol. Wherever possible, I give variations without the chocolate, however, there is another solution and that is to find sugarless chocolate that does not affect you adversely. Ross® bars seem less problematic. Place in food processor and use pulse button to coarsely chop chocolate, or weigh chocolate for amount required.

6. ***Vanilla whey protein powder*** (uses sucralose as sweetener) that I used is an inexpensive brand called R & L Health® (natural vanilla flavor) available at Costco. It comes in a 1 kg container.

7. ***Bundt pans, loaf pans and springform pans***, I usually line with wax paper and spray with nonstick cooking spray. Low-carb baking often sticks more easily to older pans. Just make sure it is neatly lined, as big folds of paper will stick into the batter and cause problems later. Brand new nonstick pans will usually not pose a problem, as long as they are well greased.

8. ***Bake Mixes:*** During the time of writing my cookbooks, I've concentrated on having various bake mixes, however, I have narrowed down my preferences with the bake mixes. Today I most commonly use Vital Oat Ultimate Bake Mix (meaning oat flour is used in the formulation), page 20 and the Low-Carb Bake Mix, page 22. Both may be used interchangeably, keeping in mind that one uses 2 tbsp (25 mL) extra Low-Carb Bake Mix for every cup of Vital Oat Ultimate Bake Mix or white flour that one is substituting. Vital Oat Ultimate Bake Mix is very tasty in a variety of recipes; however, sometimes the baked product can still have carbs that are unacceptably high for some people. Low-Carb Bake Mix is so useful as it practically guarantees a good result, as well as much lower carbs. The only flour in it is vital wheat gluten and it is 75% protein. Try these bake mixes in your own favorite recipes and enjoy great results too! Just add liquid cautiously as described. To calculate the nutritional analysis of your own recipes, there are many programs on the market, and www.fitday.com is offering one free, as well as one's own program (not on the internet) that is instantly downloadable after payment. I keep my bake mixes in labeled, transparent and airtight containers at room temperature.

9. ***Loaves (quick breads) and muffins:*** Typically, these bake a little faster due to the low-carb ingredients. Check loaf 15 minutes before first suggested baking time is completed. Cover lightly with foil if it is browning too fast. Loaves and muffins are baked when a knife inserted in the center comes out clean. Quick breads and muffins freeze well. Slice loaf and place in sealed plastic container, or wrap cooled loaf in plastic wrap and then in foil. Freeze muffins, also frosted muffins, in sealed plastic container in one layer.

10. ***Pies:*** For making piecrusts, a food processor works quickly to mix cold ingredients. Before electric appliances, butter was cut in using fingers, knives or a device called a pastry cutter. To keep baked edges of piecrust from getting too brown, cover pie lightly with foil after the first 10 minutes of baking and if the crust is pre-baked, cover with foil from the start as low-carb crusts brown very quickly. *To cover pie with foil and prevent touching filling:* fold back large piece of foil at both ends and stand these "feet" on the oven rack, effectively placing a foil tent over the pie.

11. ***Cakes:*** Usually butter and eggs should be at room temperature, although my recipes are very forgiving. If time is a factor, place eggs in a bowl in warm water and microwave butter briefly in a separate bowl. Preheat the oven and bake cake on center rack.

Low-carb baking tends to stick in pans more often. To grease and "flour" pans, generously grease bottom and sides of pans and sprinkle with bake mix. Shake pan to evenly coat and tap out any excess bake mix. Also, see #7.

Test for doneness 8 minutes prior to recipe directions for doneness. Use a toothpick to prick the center of the cake. If the toothpick comes out with just a few dry crumbs, the cake is done. If the toothpick is wet, continue to bake, checking at 2-minute intervals. If using a dinner knife instead to test for doneness, it should come out clean.

Cool layered cakes 10 minutes in pans on wire rack. Remove from pans using knife and flat, hard spatula to aid removal. Cool on wire rack. Use serrated knife to trim cake layers, if necessary, so that cakes will sit evenly. Cool tube cakes completely in the pan on a wire rack, before inverting. Let cakes cool completely before frosting, unless otherwise specified.

Unfrosted cakes last up to 3 months in the freezer if tightly wrapped. Frosted cakes should be placed unwrapped on a foil-lined cookie sheet. Freeze until hard and then wrap cake with plastic and foil. Defrost unwrapped in refrigerator.

12. **Cheesecakes:** Different brands of cream cheese vary in taste and texture, therefore find one that you prefer. Cream cheese should be at room temperature to prevent lumpy batter. Eggs should also be at room temperature. Let cream cheese and eggs sit on countertop 3 to 4 hours. If time is a factor, soften cream cheese in the microwave oven and place eggs in bowl of warm water. Do not beat cheesecake batter too long to prevent air bubbles from getting into the batter. Add eggs one at a time while processing and just until incorporated. If your springform pan is old, cover bottom with wax paper and clamp ring in place. Trim wax paper with scissors. Spray inside of springform pan with nonstick cooking spray. The firmer cheesecakes, when thoroughly chilled, can be lifted right off the springform pan bottom onto a cake stand. Another pan that is wonderful is a nonstick cheesecake pan with a bottom that pops up similar to a tart pan bottom. This type of pan usually does not need greasing or wax paper.

The cheesecake should be set about 2 inches (5 cm) or a bit more from circumference to center of cheesecake. Center will be soft and jiggly. This produces a silky, smooth cheesecake, however, my husband's preference is for a firm cheesecake and to achieve this, I bake cheesecakes until the center is just softly set and it is turning light brown at the outer edges with a few cracks also forming at the outer edges. If the cheesecake is firmly set in the center it is overbaked. Do not jar cake during removal and cooling. Run a thin knife between cheesecake and pan while it is still hot. Remove ring of springform pan after cheesecake has cooled or after a day to prevent a tinny taste being imparted. Cover with plastic wrap and refrigerate.

Splendid Low-Carb Desserts

To serve, use a very sharp, thin knife dipped in hot water. Wrap cheesecake in plastic wrap and foil and freeze for up to 3 months. Defrost approximately 24 hours in refrigerator. Garnish and chill. Beautiful cheesecakes are typically decorated cheesecakes and most times I give some garnishing ideas.

13.   **Cookies and Squares:** It is better to bake only one baking sheet of cookies at a time in the oven for best results, however, if time is a factor and you'd like to bake two sheets at a time, rotate the baking sheets halfway through baking time. Make sure the baking sheets do not touch the back or sides of the oven. Bake squares in center of oven. Check cookies and squares after minimum suggested baking time. Cookies are usually stored at room temperature in an airtight container. Cookies and most squares can be frozen in airtight containers or freezer bags up to 4 months. Crisp cookies will freeze better than soft ones. Thaw cookies and brownies unwrapped at room temperature.

14.   **Ice Creams:** A tip to avoid ice crystals: Add 3 tsp (15 mL) unflavored gelatin per 6 cups (1.5 L) of ice cream mixture. Let the gelatin soften in 1/4 cup (50 mL) of the mixture, then gently heat it until it is dissolved. Add to the remaining mixture and freeze according to manufacturer's instructions. Faster freezing ensures a smoother ice cream. The temperature of the mix when freezing determines how fast freezing takes place. A starting temperature between 30°F (-1°C) and 35°F (2°C) works well. If the mixture is very warm, there is a risk of the cream being churned into butter. Store ice cream covered in freezer, so that it does not absorb flavors from other foods.

My ice cream maker is a modern one with a metal canister that one freezes. I simply store my canister in the freezer, and when I want to make ice cream, it is freezing cold and ready to go. There is no running to the store to get ice or rock salt and no crank to turn, although the capacity is less than the old fashioned ones. Transfer the finished ice cream to a sealed container in the freezer to harden for 2 to 4 hours. It is a necessary part of making ice cream, however, I can hardly wait, and so I often enjoy the soft serve ice cream.

DEDICATION: This book took approximately 4 months and a bit to create, edit and get ready for publishing. It was a fun project and would never have seen the light of day had I not received my inspiration from God and received the support from my loving family. I would not feel happy sharing this book with you, without also sharing that God saw me through several difficult and heartbreaking trials in my life. Our family witnessed several miracles and many answers to prayer. I firmly believe I could not have completed any of my cookbooks without God in my life. *This is how wonderful God is to His creation here on earth:*
John 3:16: "For God so loved the world, that He sent His only begotten Son to die for us, that whosoever believes in Him shall not perish but have everlasting life."

BEVERAGES

MINT TRUFFLE COCOA

Great for one of those cold, wintry nights in front of a roaring fire.

1 tbsp Hot Chocolate Drink Mix, (15 mL)
  page 9
1 tbsp Da Vinci® Sugar Free (15 mL)
  Chocolate Syrup
1 tbsp Da Vinci® Sugar Free (15 mL)
  Crème de Menthe or Peppermint Paddy
  Syrup
1$^1/_2$ tsp whipping cream (7 mL)

> **Yield:** 1 serving
> 1 serving
> 36.6 calories
> 1.2 g protein
> 2.5 g fat
> **2.5 g carbs**

In coffee cup, combine Hot Chocolate Drink Mix, page 9, Da Vinci® Sugar Free Chocolate Syrup and Da Vinci® Sugar Free Crème de Menthe or Peppermint Paddy Syrup. Using tiny wire whisk, combine well. Add water almost to top of cup. Microwave 1 minute on high power. Add cream; whisk again. Microwave 20 seconds more. Enjoy!

Variations: **Da Vinci® Alternative:** Use 2 tbsp (25 mL) Hot Chocolate Drink Mix, page 9 and 3 tiny drops mint and peppermint extract, or to taste. (**4.9 g Carbs**)

Kahlua Hot Cocoa: Replace Da Vinci® Sugar Free Crème De Menthe or Peppermint Paddy Syrup with Da Vinci® Sugar Free Kahuli Caffe Syrup. (**2.5 g Carbs**)

Helpful Hint: For a richer cup of hot chocolate, use 2 tbsp (25 mL) Hot Chocolate Drink Mix, page 9 and extra cream, if desired.

~~Low-Carb Dieting Tip~~
Focus on your low-carb diet one day at a time.

HOT CHOCOLATE DRINK MIX

This drink mix is a little sweeter than the one in Splendid Low-Carbing. Often this drink is all that is needed as a sweet ending to a meal or to help soothe chocolate cravings. Take the drink mix on vacations!

$1^2/_3$ cups skim, OR whole milk (400 mL)
  powder
1 cup SPLENDA® Granular (250 mL)
35 SPLENDA® packets
$^2/_3$ cup Dutch cocoa (150 mL)
$^1/_8$ tsp salt, OR to taste (0.5 mL)

Yield: $3^1/_2$ cup (875 mL)
1 tbsp (15 mL) per serving
14.2 calories
1.0 g protein
0.1 g fat
2.3 g carbs

In large plastic container with lid, combine skim or whole milk powder, SPLENDA® Granular, SPLENDA®, Dutch cocoa and salt. Stir well. Seal container with lid and shake vigorously to further combine.

How to serve: Use 2 tbsp (25 mL) Hot Chocolate Drink Mix in a mug. Stir in $1^1/_2$ tsp (7 mL) to 1 tbsp (15 mL) whipping cream, using a tiny whisk, to form a paste. Fill the rest of the mug with water. Microwave one minute on high power. Whisk again. Add 1 tbsp (15 mL) Da Vinci® Sugar Free Kahuli Caffe Syrup or any other flavor of choice for lifting this hot chocolate drink to a new level. Microwave 30 seconds more. (*4.8 g Carbs*)

Helpful Hint: One may use only 1 tbsp (15 mL) Hot Chocolate Drink Mix if using even 1 tbsp (15 mL) Da Vinci® Sugar Free Syrup of choice. (*2.5 g Carbs*)

COCONUT MILK SHAKE

A taste of the tropics.

3 cups plain yogurt (750 mL)
1 cup coconut milk (250 mL)
$^1/_2$ cup SPLENDA® Granular (125 mL)
$^1/_4$ cup Da Vinci® Sugar Free (50 mL)
  Coconut Syrup, OR coconut extract
  to taste and water

Yield: $4^1/_2$ cups (1.125 L)
$^1/_2$ cup (125 mL) per serving
112.1 calories
4.0 g protein
8.0 g fat
3.4 g carbs

In blender, combine yogurt, coconut milk, SPLENDA® Granular and Da Vinci® Sugar Free Coconut Syrup or coconut extract and water.

ICED CAFFE LATTE

A very popular, refreshing drink, but it usually has more than 20 g of carbohydrate per serving. This Iced Caffe Latte is decarbed for your pleasure.

2 tbsp Hot Chocolate Drink Mix, (25 mL)
  page 9
3 rounded tsp instant coffee (20 mL)
2 SPLENDA® packets, or to taste
$^1/_4$ cup boiling water (50 mL)
$2^1/_2$ cups ice cold water (625 mL)
$^3/_4$ cup cup whipping cream (175 mL)

Yield: 3 generous servings
1 serving
90.2 calories
2.6 g protein
6.6 g fat
5.4 g carbs

In jug, combine Hot Chocolate Drink Mix, page 9, instant coffee and SPLENDA®. Gradually, stir in boiling water. When no trace of coffee granules remains, stir in ice cold water and whipping cream. Serve over ice.

Helpful Hints: Decaffeinated coffee granules may be used. My teeenage son, Jonathan, found this drink lovely, but not sweet enough for his taste. He added an extra SPLENDA® packet to his Iced Caffe Latte and was quite happy!

WHITE HOT CHOCOLATE

This is a fun comfort drink – different! Everyone in the family likes it.

1 tbsp Confectioner's Sugar (15 mL)
  Substitute, page 65
2 tbsp Da Vinci® Sugar Free (25 mL)
  White Chocolate Syrup
$1^1/_2$ tsp whipping cream (7 mL)

Yield: 1 cup (250 mL)
1 serving
42.2 calories
1.5 g protein
3.1 g fat
2.1 g carbs

In teacup, place Confectioner's Sugar Substitute, page 65. Gradually stir in Da Vinci® Sugar Free White Chocolate Syrup and whipping cream. Stir in water to fill cup and microwave 115 seconds. Enjoy!

~~Low-Carb Dieting Tip~~
Yogurt is reported to help weight loss. See page 14, Splendid Low-Carbing.

STRAWBERRY BANANA SMOOTHIE

Fruit and yogurt is a good start to the morning, when insulin is more sensitive.

1 cup frozen strawberries, (250 mL)
  (unsweetened)
1 cup plain yogurt (250 mL)
$^1/_2$ cup SPLENDA® Granular (125 mL)
$^1/_4$ cup Da Vinci® Sugar Free (50 mL)
  Banana Syrup

> **Yield:** 2 cups (500 mL)
> $^1/_2$ cup (125 mL) per serving
> 68.0 calories
> 2.8 g protein
> 2.0 g fat
> **6.6 g carbs**

In blender, combine strawberries, yogurt, SPLENDA® Granular and Da Vinci® Sugar Free Banana Syrup. Blend until smooth.

Variations: Use any combination of fruit and Da Vinci® Sugar Free Syrup to make your own flavor combinations of this delicious, thick smoothie.

Da Vinci® Alternative: Use 1 tsp (5 mL) banana extract and $^1/_4$ cup (50 mL) extra yogurt (***7.0 g Carbs***), or use water for no increase in carbs, unless you need to add one packet of SPLENDA® for extra sweetness.

PEACH YOGURT SHAKE

Very peachy!

2 cups plain yogurt (500 mL)
$^3/_4$ cup canned sliced peaches (175 mL)
  in juice, drained
$^1/_2$ cup SPLENDA® Granular (125 mL)
$^1/_4$ cup Da Vinci® Sugar Free (50 mL)
  Peach or Vanilla Syrup

> **Yield:** 3 cups (750 mL)
> $^1/_2$ cup (125 mL) per serving
> 72.6 calories
> 3.6 g protein
> 2.7 g fat
> **4.9 g carbs**

In blender, combine yogurt, peaches, SPLENDA® Granular and Da Vinci® Sugar Free Peach or Vanilla Syrup. Blend until smooth.

Variations: **Spiced Pear Yogurt Shake:** Use canned pear halves, in juice and drained. Use Da Vinci® Sugar Free Ginger or Cinnamon Syrup. (***5.1 g Carbs***)

Da Vinci® Alternative: Substitute 2 tbsp (25 mL) whipping cream plus 2 tbsp (25 mL) water. Add 1 SPLENDA® packet and 1 tsp (5 mL) vanilla extract. (***5.3 g Carbs***)

BAKE MIXES, LOAVES & MUFFINS

PUMPKIN CHIP MUFFINS

These are good served slightly warm or at room temperature. Microwave cooled muffins briefly to warm, if desired.

4 eggs
2 cups SPLENDA® Granular (500 mL)
$^3/_4$ cup olive oil (175 mL)
$^3/_4$ cup canned pumpkin (175 mL)
$^1/_4$ cup whipping cream (50 mL)
$3^1/_3$ cups Low-Carb Bake Mix, (825 mL)
  page 22
2 tsp baking powder (10 mL)
$1^1/_2$ tsp baking soda (7 mL)
1 tsp cinnamon (5 mL)
$^1/_2$ tsp salt (2 mL)
2 cups sugarless chocolate chips (500 mL)
  (sweetened)

Yield: 24 muffins
1 muffin
223.3 calories
7.7 g protein
16.2 g fat
4.9 g carbs

In large bowl, beat eggs with fork. Stir in SPLENDA® Granular, olive oil, pumpkin and whipping cream. In another large bowl, combine Low-Carb Bake Mix, page 22, baking powder, baking soda, cinnamon and salt. Stir in chocolate chips. Pour pumpkin mixture into well in dry ingredients and stir just until combined.

Fill 24 large, paper-lined or greased muffin cups $^2/_3$ cup full. Bake in 400°F (200°C) oven 12 to 15 minutes, or until muffins test done with toothpick coming out clean (try to avoid chocolate chips).

Variations: **Pumpkin Pecan Muffins:** Use 2 cups (500 mL) chopped pecans instead of sugarless chocolate chips. (*5.2 g Carbs*)

Pumpkin Pecan Chip Muffins: Use 1 cup (250 mL) chopped pecans and 1 cup (250 mL) sugarless chocolate chips. (*5.0 g Carbs*)

Helpful Hints: These muffins freeze well. Place in plastic container with lid in single layer and freeze up to 3 months. Microwave 55 seconds, butter and enjoy, or better yet allow to defrost overnight in refrigerator.

LEMONY DELIGHT MUFFINS

My husband loved the light texture of these lower calorie muffins.

$2^1/_4$ cups Low-Carb Bake Mix, (550 mL)
  page 22
$^3/_4$ cup SPLENDA® Granular (175 mL)
1 tsp baking powder (5 mL)
$^1/_2$ tsp baking soda (2 mL)
$^1/_4$ tsp salt (1 mL)
2 eggs
1 cup plain yogurt, OR (250 mL)
  sour cream
3 tbsp butter, melted (45 mL)
2 tbsp lemon juice (25 mL)
1 tbsp finely grated lemon peel (15 mL)
Lemony Glaze:
3 tbsp lemon juice (45 mL)
3 tbsp SPLENDA® Granular (45 mL)
$^1/_8$ tsp Thickening Agent, page 66 (0.5 mL)

Yield: 12 muffins
1 muffin
154.2 calories
10.1 g protein
10.2 g fat
4.7 g carbs

In large bowl, combine Low-Carb Bake Mix, page 22, SPLENDA® Granular, baking powder, baking soda and salt. In another bowl, whisk eggs. Whisk in yogurt, butter, lemon juice and grated lemon peel. Add to a well in dry ingredients and combine just until moist. Fill 12 paper-lined or greased muffin cups almost to the top. Bake in 400°F (200°C) oven 15 to 20 minutes, or until tops are turning golden brown and cake tester comes out clean. Using pastry brush, brush glaze on each muffin.

Lemony Glaze: In small saucepan, combine lemon juice, SPLENDA® Granular and Thickening Agent, page 66. Bring to boil.

~~Low-Carb Dieting Tip~~
If you begin stressing over weighing on the scale each day, skip a few days, be extra good and weigh again.

BLUEBERRY MUFFINS

Lovely muffins chock full of blueberries. See lower carb variation below.

3 cups Vital Oat Ultimate (750 mL)
  Bake Mix, page 20
1 cup SPLENDA® Granular (250 mL)
2 tbsp baking powder (25 mL)
$^1/_2$ tsp salt (2 mL)
2 cups frozen blueberries (500 mL)
  (unsweetened)
$^2/_3$ cup butter, softened (150 mL)
2 extra large eggs
$^1/_2$ cup whipping cream (125 mL)
$^1/_2$ cup water (125 mL)
2 tsp vanilla extract (10 mL)

Yield: 18 muffins
1 muffin
184.5 calories
6.4 g protein
15.2 g fat
7.5 g carbs

In large bowl, combine Vital Oat Ultimate Bake Mix, page 20, SPLENDA® Granular, baking powder and salt. Stir in blueberries.

In food processor with sharp blade, process butter. Add eggs, whipping cream, water and vanilla extract; process. Stir into dry ingredients, just until moist.

Fill 18 greased muffin cups $^2/_3$ full and bake 20 minutes in 375°F (190°C) oven. After a day, refrigerate muffins. Warm slightly in microwave oven before serving.

Variation: "Cornmeal" Blueberry Muffins: Use 3 cups (750 mL) plus 6 tbsp (90 mL) Low-Carb Bake Mix, page 22. These taste almost as though there is cornmeal in the muffins. (***5.6 g Carbs***)

Helpful Hints: These muffins freeze well. Using all-purpose flour in the Vital Ultimate Bake Mix, page 20 produces tender, cake-like muffins (***9.1 g Carbs***). Jonathan said these were better than the regular higher carb blueberry muffins from Splendid Desserts.

~~Low-Carb Dieting Tip~~
Make your goal weight realistic. Don't set yourself up for failure.

APPLESAUCE CARROT MUFFINS

A healthy and fairly large muffin that tastes lovely buttered. Only flour in each muffin is $^1/_2$ tbsp (7 mL) vital wheat gluten which is 75% protein.

$1^1/_2$ cups ground almonds (375 mL)
$^3/_4$ cup vanilla whey protein (175 mL)
6 tbsp vital wheat gluten (90 mL)
2 tsp baking powder (10 mL)
1 tsp cinnamon (5 mL)
$^1/_4$ tsp salt (1 mL)
$^1/_2$ cup finely grated carrot (125 mL)
$^1/_4$ cup chopped walnuts, OR (50 mL)
  pecans
2 extra-large eggs
$^3/_4$ cup unsweetened applesauce (175 mL)
$^1/_3$ cup olive oil (75 mL)
Cream Cheese Frosting, page 46
  (optional)

> *Yield:* 12 muffins
> 1 muffin
> 214.4 calories
> 11.6 g protein
> 16.3 g fat
> *5.4 g carbs*

In large bowl, combine ground almonds, vanilla whey protein, vital wheat gluten, baking powder, cinnamon and salt. Stir in grated carrot and chopped walnuts or pecans. In small bowl, beat eggs with fork. Stir in unsweetened applesauce and olive oil. Add to dry ingredients and stir just until combined.

Fill 12 greased muffin cups $^2/_3$ full and bake 15 minutes in 375°F (190°C) oven, or until slightly browned and cake tester comes out clean.

Cream Cheese Frosting (if using): Prepare as directed on page 46. Frost cooled muffins.

Variation: **Applesauce Zucchini Muffins:** Replace grated carrot with grated zucchini. (*5.2 g Carbs*)

Helpful Hints: These muffins are great with sliced Cheddar cheese for breakfast. They freeze well in a sealed plastic container for at least 2 months. They are really special with Cream cheese Frosting, page 46. (*6.5 g Carbs*)

~~Low-Carb Dieting Tip~~
Losing pounds on the scale is not everything. Gaining muscle will show up as a gain on the scale, however, more muscle means a faster metabolism.

TOASTED COCONUT LOAF

A dense-textured, high fiber loaf that is good spread with Healthy Butter or Spreadable Cream Cheese, pages 53 and 60 respectively in Splendid Low-Carbing for Life, Vol. 1

$1^1/_4$ cups desiccated coconut, (300 mL)
$2^1/_4$ cups Low-Carb Bake Mix, (550 mL)
  page 22
1 cup SPLENDA® Granular (250 mL)
2 tsp baking powder (10 mL)
$^1/_4$ tsp salt (1 mL)
2 eggs, lightly whisked
$^1/_2$ cup water (125 mL)
$^1/_4$ cup whipping cream (50 mL)
$^1/_4$ cup olive oil (50 mL)
$2^1/_2$ tsp vanilla extract (12 mL)
2 tsp coconut extract (10 mL)

Yield: 18 slices
1 slice
149.9 calories
6.4 g protein
11.2 g fat
5.3 g carbs

Spread coconut out on baking sheet. Bake in 350°F (180°C) oven 4 or 5 minutes. Remove and stir coconut until all coconut is mixed well and golden in color. In large bowl, combine Low-Carb Bake Mix, page 22, SPLENDA® Granular, baking powder and salt. Stir in coconut. In small bowl, combine eggs, water, cream, olive oil, vanilla and coconut extracts. Whisk together.

To a well in center of dry ingredients, add egg mixture. Stir until moistened. Pour into a greased wax paper-lined 9 x 5 x 3-inch (2 L) loaf pan. Bake in 350°F (180°C) oven 40 to 50 minutes, or until knife inserted in center comes out clean. Cover loaf lightly with foil, if browning too much.

Helpful Hint: Do set timer to prevent burning the coconut while toasting it in the oven.

~~Low-Carb Dieting Tip~~
Yeast, food intolerances and thyroid problems can cause very slow weight loss or halt it altogether.

APPLE CINNAMON SWIRL LOAF

Wonderful, flavorful loaf.

$2^{1}/_{4}$ cups Low-Carb Bake Mix, (550 mL)
  page 22, OR
2 cups Vital Oat Ultimate Bake, (500 mL)
  page 20
1 cup SPLENDA® Granular (250 mL)
2 tsp baking powder (10 mL)
$^{1}/_{2}$ tsp baking soda (2 mL)
$1^{1}/_{2}$ tsp cinnamon (7 mL)
$^{1}/_{2}$ tsp salt (2 mL)
2 extra-large eggs
$^{1}/_{2}$ cup whipping cream (125 mL)
$^{1}/_{3}$ cup olive oil (75 mL)
$^{1}/_{3}$ cup unsweetened applesauce (75 mL)
1 tsp vanilla extract (5 mL)
Topping:
2 tbsp SPLENDA® Granular (25 mL)
1 tbsp Low-Carb Bake Mix, page 22 (15 mL)
  OR Vital Oat Ultimate Bake Mix, 20
1 tsp cinnamon (5 mL)
2 tsp butter (10 mL)

Yield: 18 servings
1 serving LCBM/VOUBM
141.9/139.5 calories
6.7/4.6 g protein
11.1/10.9 g fat
3.8/5.3 g carbs

In large bowl, combine Low-Carb Bake Mix, page 22, or Vital Oat Ultimate Bake Mix, page 20, SPLENDA® Granular, baking powder, baking soda, cinnamon and salt. In small bowl, beat eggs with fork. Stir in whipping cream, olive oil, applesauce and vanilla extract. Add to dry ingredients and stir just until combined. Sprinkle topping over loaf and using knife swirl it into batter. Bake in 350°F (180°C) oven 30 to 35 minutes, or until cake tester inserted in loaf comes out clean and loaf is slightly brown. Cool on wire rack 10 minutes. Remove.

Topping: In small bowl, combine SPLENDA® Granular, Low-Carb Bake Mix, page 22, or Vital Oat Ultimate Bake Mix, page 20 and cinnamon. Rub in butter.

Helpful Hints: This loaf is moist with both bake mixes. It is more dense in texture with the Low-Carb Bake Mix, page 22, and fluffier with the Vital Oat Ultimate Bake Mix, page 20. We liked them both. Perhaps, though, if I were to serve it to guests, I would use the Vital Oat Ultimate Bake Mix, simply because it more closely resembles the texture one would get with all-purpose flour, and not necessarily because it is nicer. Leftover applesauce freezes very well.

FAVORITE BANANA BREAD

There is real banana in this loaf! Also see Frosted Banana Loaf, Splendid Low-Carbing, page 127.

8 oz regular cream cheese, (250 g)
  softened
$1^1/_4$ cups SPLENDA® Granular (300 mL)
$^1/_4$ cup butter (50 mL)
2 tbsp olive oil (25 mL)
$1^1/_2$ tsp banana extract (7 mL)
2 eggs
$^2/_3$ cup mashed banana (150 mL)
$2^1/_2$ cups Low-Carb Bake Mix, (625 mL)
  page 22
2 tsp baking powder (10 mL)
$^1/_2$ tsp baking soda (2 mL)
Orange Cheese Frosting, page 72 (optional)

Yield: 18 slices
1 slice
169.1 calories
8.1 g protein
12.9 g fat
5.4 g carbs

In food processor with sharp blade or in bowl with electric mixer, process cream cheese until smooth. Add SPLENDA® Granular, butter, olive oil, banana extract and eggs; process. Add banana and process briefly.

In medium bowl, combine Low-Carb Bake Mix, page 22, baking powder and baking soda. Add to banana mixture and process just until combined and moistened.

Line 9 x 5 x 3-inch (2 L) loaf pan with wax paper and spray with nonstick cooking spray. Pour batter into loaf pan and smooth out surface. Bake in 350°F (180°C) oven 1 hour and 10 minutes, or until knife inserted in center of loaf comes out clean. After 30 minutes of baking, cover loaf lightly with foil, as it will already be golden brown. Continue to bake until done as described. Remove loaf, peel wax paper off sides and let cool on wire rack. If desired, spread delicious *Orange Cheese Frosting, page 72* over top of completely cooled loaf for a truly delicious taste experience. (*6.8 g Carbs*)

Helpful Hints: This loaf may sink ever so slightly upon cooling, due to the high moisture content. To minimize this, do not underbake loaf and use a flat dinner knife to test for doneness.

~~Low-Carb Dieting Tip~~
Studies show that nuts provide rich nutrients and lower incidence of heart attack.

CAKE DONUTS

These won't last long. According to my family, they prefer the deep-fried version, however, I was just as happy with the lower calorie version.

2 cups Vital Oat Ultimate Bake (500 mL)
  Mix, page 20
$^3/_4$ cup SPLENDA® Granular (175 mL)
$1^3/_4$ tsp baking powder (8 mL)
$^1/_4$ tsp salt (1 mL)
$^1/_4$ tsp nutmeg (1 mL)
$^1/_4$ tsp cinnamon (1 mL)
2 eggs
$^1/_2$ cup Da Vinci® Sugar Free
  French Vanilla, OR Cookie Dough Syrup (125 mL)
$^1/_4$ cup half-and-half cream (50 mL)
1 tsp vanilla extract (5 mL)
Icing:
$^3/_4$ cup Confectioner's Sugar Substitute, (175 mL)
  page 65
3 tbsp Da Vinci® Sugar Free French Vanilla, (45 mL)
  OR Cookie Dough Syrup
2 tbsp butter, melted (25 mL)

Yield: 22 Cake Donuts
1 Donut
90.7 calories
4.5 g protein
5.8 g fat
4.6 g carbs

In large bowl, combine Vital Oat Ultimate Bake Mix, page 20, SPLENDA® Granular, baking powder, salt, nutmeg and cinnamon. In medium bowl, whisk together eggs, Da Vinci® Sugar Free French Vanilla or Cookie Dough Syrup, half-and-half cream and vanilla extract. Add to dry ingredients, stirring until moist. Spray nonstick mini donut pan with cooking spray. Fill each donut hole with batter, about $^2/_3$ full. Bake in 325°F (160°C) oven 10 to 12 minutes, or until tops spring back when lightly touched. Dip tops in icing. Before dipping donuts, if desired, deep fry in hot oil until turning golden. Remove and dip in icing.

Icing: In small bowl, whisk together Confectioner's Sugar Substitute, page 65, Da Vinci® Sugar Free French Vanilla or Cookie Dough Syrup and butter.

Variations: Lower Carb Alternative: Use chilled zero carb thick commercial syrup (***3.3 g Carbs***) to dip hot, fried donuts in.

Da Vinci® Alternative: Substitute $^1/_2$ cup (125 mL) whipping cream for half-and-half cream and $^1/_4$ cup (50 mL) water for Da Vinci® Sugar Free Syrup. If desired, increase sweetener slightly. (***4.7 g Carbs***)

VITAL ULTIMATE BAKE MIX

Substitute cup-for-cup for all-purpose flour. Regular sugar and white flour recipes will have carbs reduced by about 60 %, if SPLENDA® is used as well.

Vital Ultimate Bake Mix (with spelt):
$1^1/_2$ cups ground almonds, OR (375 mL)
   ground hazelnuts, pecans or walnuts
1 cup spelt, OR all-purpose, (250 mL)
   whole wheat pastry flour, OR
   oat flour* (last two have fewer carbs)
$^1/_2$ cup vital wheat gluten (125 mL)

> **Yield:** 3 cups (750 mL)
> $^1/_4$ cup (50 mL)/serv. (spelt)
> 139.5 calories
> 8.2 g protein
> 8.0 g fat
> **8.4 g carbs**

In medium bowl, combine ground almonds (hazelnuts, pecans or walnuts), spelt flour (all-purpose, whole wheat pastry or oat flour) and vital wheat gluten; stir well. Substitute cup-for-cup for all-purpose flour. With all bake mixes, add liquid in your own recipes very cautiously, withholding $^1/_4$ cup (50 mL) to $^1/_2$ cup (125 mL) and adding it as necessary.

Variations: *Vital Whole Wheat Ultimate Bake Mix: (using the same formulation in main recipe, only with whole wheat pastry flour):
131.4 calories, 7.8 g protein, 7.9 g fat, **6.9 g carbs**.

***Vital Oat Ultimate Bake Mix:** (using the same formulation in main recipe, only with oat flour): 136.5 calories, 8.1 g protein, 8.3 g fat, **6.1 g carbs**.

Vital Ultimate Bake Mix (with all-purpose flour): I very rarely use this combination, but will choose to make the bake mix with spelt flour instead as in main recipe with nutritional analysis shown.
144.1 calories, 7.9 g protein, 7.9 g fat, **9.7 g carbs**.

Helpful Hints: The ground almonds, all-purpose flour and vital wheat gluten combination in Vital Ultimate Bake Mix is very similar to regular baking and often better, producing lovely, moist baked goods and is particularly useful for delicate cakes that require a tender crumb texture. Spelt flour (a complex carbohydrate flour not biologically related to wheat flour – for those who are allergic to wheat flour) will be almost as good in such instances. Please see Helpful Hints, page 5, for more information on bake mixes and their application.

~~Low-Carb Dieting Tip~~
When your body is burning alcohol, it will not burn fat.

NUT-FREE ULTIMATE BAKE MIX

For those who are allergic to nuts, this works well as an alternative to the ultimate bake mixes, page 20. This bake mix may be substituted cup-for-cup for all-purpose flour or for my ultimate bake mixes. See below for instructions on replacing Low-Carb Bake Mix, page 22 with this bake mix.

$^2/_3$ cup whole wheat pastry flour (150 mL)
$^1/_2$ cup vital wheat gluten (125 mL)
$^1/_2$ cup vanilla whey protein, OR (125 mL)
  natural whey protein powder
$^1/_2$ cup ground flax seeds, (125 mL)
$^1/_3$ cup spelt, OR all-purpose, OR (75 mL)
  whole wheat pastry flour

Yield: $2^1/_2$ cups (625 mL)
$^1/_4$ cup (50 ml) per serving
96.5 calories
10.3 g protein
2.2 g fat
7.7 g carbs

In large bowl, combine whole wheat pastry flour, vital wheat gluten, vanilla whey protein or natural whey protein, ground flax seeds and spelt, all-purpose or whole wheat pastry flour. Mix well. Add liquid in your recipe cautiously, withholding $^1/_4$ cup (50 mL) to $^1/_2$ cup (125 mL) liquid, and adding only as necessary, until the correct consistency is achieved.

Variation: **Nut-Free Oat Ultimate Bake Mix:** Substitute 1 cup (250 mL) oat flour, $^1/_2$ cup (125 mL) vital wheat gluten, $^1/_2$ cup (125 mL) vanilla whey protein and $^1/_2$ cup (125 mL) ground flax seeds. *Yield:* $2^1/_2$ cups (625 mL)
$^1/_4$ cup (50 ml) per serving: 99.3 calories, 10.5 g protein, 2.7 g fat, *6.3 g carbs*

Helpful Hints: This bake mix is very good in muffins and loaves, coffee cakes and many cookies, however, with more refined, delicate cakes, it may be better to switch the amounts for the whole wheat pastry flour and spelt or all-purpose flour around: (*8.4 g Carbs*) using spelt flour. On the other hand in the main recipe, for some muffins and loaves, it is possible to use only whole wheat pastry flour and omit spelt flour or all-purpose flour. (*7.2 g Carbs*)

I tried using 1 cup (250 mL) of vanilla whey protein in this Nut-free Ultimate Bake Mix; however, baked goods were very dry. The flax seeds solve that problem nicely. Typically, this bake mix will require about the same amount of liquid as your regular recipe calls for, however, it is better to take the cautious route as described in the recipe instructions, just in case. Natural whey protein powder should be used in applications, where extra sweetness in the vanilla whey protein powder would be a problem.

When replacing Low-Carb Bake Mix, page 22 in recipes, use 2 tbsp (25 mL) less per cup (250 mL).

LOW-CARB BAKE MIX

This tasty bake mix guarantees a low-carb result in your baking. Regular sugar and white flour recipes will have carbs reduced by about 85%, if Low-Carb Bake Mix is substituted for white flour and SPLENDA® Granular is used to substitute for sugar as well, and this is without taking into account changing other items in the recipe for low-carb ones.

$1^2/_3$ cups ground almonds (400 mL)
$^2/_3$ cup vanilla whey protein* (150 mL)
$^2/_3$ cup vital wheat gluten (150 mL)

Yield: $3^1/_3$ cups (825 mL)
$^1/_3$ cup (75 mL) per serving
162.9 calories
14.3 g protein
10.3 g fat
3.3 g carbs

In large bowl, combine ground almonds, vanilla whey protein and vital wheat gluten. Use a large wooden spoon to stir and mix well. See Helpful Hints below for instructions on how to use this bake mix. Store in a closed container at room temperature. Shake container to ensure ingredients are combined well.

Helpful Hints: For some strange reason, the total yield for this bake mix is $^1/_3$ cup (75 mL) more than the 3 cups (750 mL) one would expect. One ingredient tends to fluff up when they're mixed together is my best guess. If one chooses to see the yield as 3 cups (750 mL), the carbs increase slightly to 3.7 g.

To use this bake mix: Typically, for every cup of flour in your recipe, replace with 1 cup (250 mL) of Low-Carb Bake Mix, plus 2 tbsp (25 mL). The aforementioned rules apply also to replacing any of the Ultimate Bake Mixes from my previous cookbooks (which are a cup-for-cup substitution for all-purpose flour) as well as Vital Ultimate Bake Mixes, page 20 with this bake mix.

Once again, always add liquid cautiously to your own recipes that you wish to de-carb. Sometimes as much as $^1/_2$ cup (125 mL) less wet ingredients (this includes ingredients such as butter, olive oil, applesauce, pumpkin, water, yogurt, sour cream, cream, etc.) will be required. Typically, it is $^1/_4$ cup (50 mL) wet ingredients that will need to be omitted from your regular recipe.

This bake mix produces wonderful, moist baked goods most of the time, despite the whey content. Useful for piecrusts, muffins, loaves, many cakes, cookies and squares and is guaranteed to lower carbs significantly in your favorite recipes!

*If the application for this bake mix is for a savory baked product, it is possible to replace vanilla whey protein powder with natural whey protein powder.

FROZEN DESSERTS, POPSICLES & PUDDINGS

BREAD PUDDING

An easy recipe for those times when there is not a whole lot in the pantry.

2$^1/_2$ cups dry bread cubes (625 mL)
  (about 3 ½ slices low-carb bread –
  about 5 grams carbs per slice)
2 tbsp raisins (25 mL)
4 eggs
1 cup whipping cream (250 mL)
1 cup water (250 mL)
$^1/_3$ cup SPLENDA® Granular (75 mL)
1 tbsp Da Vinci® Sugar Free (15 mL)
  French Vanilla Syrup, OR your choice,
  OR 2 tsp vanilla extract (10 mL)
$^1/_2$ tsp cinnamon (2 mL)
$^1/_4$ tsp salt (1 mL)

Yield: 6 servings
1 serving
171.9 calories
6.7 g protein
13.3 g fat
6.3 g carbs

In 2-quart (2 L) casserole dish, place bread cubes and raisins. In medium bowl, beat eggs with wire whisk. Add whipping cream, water, SPLENDA® Granular, Da Vinci® Sugar Free French Vanilla Syrup or vanilla extract, cinnamon and salt. Whisk. Pour egg mixture over bread and raisins.

Bake in 350°F (180°C) oven 30 minutes, or until set.

Helpful Hint: The nutritional analysis is based on the Wholegrain bread using whole wheat flour in *More Splendid Low-Carbing*, page 66.

~~Low-Carb Dieting Tip~~
A plateau is described as weight loss stopping for at least a month. Plateaus happen in later stages of weight loss. Count carbs more strictly and increase exercise, if possible. Keep a food journal.

PEACHES AND CREAM TRIFLE

This is a particularly easy trifle to assemble, once the pound cakes are baked.
Very tasty and always an elegant comfort dessert!

1 Mini Sour Cream Pound Cake,
  page 44, sliced thinly
$^1/_2$ cup Da Vinci® Sugar (125 mL)
  Free Peach Syrup
$^1/_4$ cup water (50 mL)
2$^1/_2$ cups sliced peaches, (625 mL)
  canned in juice, drained
1 cup whipping cream (250 mL)
$^1/_4$ cup SPLENDA® Granular (50 mL)
$^3/_4$ oz flaked almonds, toasted (25 g)
Mascarpone Cheese Substitute:
8 oz regular cream cheese, softened (250 g)
$^1/_4$ cup whipping cream (50 mL)
3 tbsp sour cream (45 mL)

Yield: 10 servings
1 serving
294.9 calories
8.3 g protein
25.6 g fat
8.2 g carbs

In trifle bowl, layer pound cake. Pour a mixture of Da Vinci® Sugar Free Peach Syrup and the water over cake slices. Layer peach slices over cake.

Mascarpone Cheese Substitute: In food processor with sharp blade, blender or in bowl with electric mixer, process cream cheese until smooth. Add whipping cream and sour cream; process. Remove and set aside. Clean bowl and dry.

In food processor, in clean, dry bowl, with whipping assembly, whip cream and SPLENDA® Granular until stiff. Add Mascarpone substitute and process briefly, to just mix. Spread over peaches. Sprinkle with flaked, toasted almonds. Refrigerate at least one hour and preferably a few hours to allow flavors to develop.

Helpful Hints: To toast almonds: In dry, nonstick skillet, toast almonds over medium heat until light golden brown. I used a fabulous substitute for Mascarpone Cheese (although you may use the real thing too), because it is very expensive and not necessarily always available at your local grocery store.

~~Low-Carb Dieting Tip~~
DHEA supplements can reduce insulin resistance and stave off diabetes. It is probably wise to get one's DHEA levels tested first and to take the smallest dose possible.

CAKE PUDDING

Definitely comfort food! There is plenty of sauce with the pudding.

1 Mini Sour Cream Pound Cake,
  page 44, sliced
2 eggs
$1^1/_2$ cups Da Vinci® Sugar Free (375 mL)
  Dulce De Leche Syrup, OR your choice
1 cup whipping cream (250 mL)
$^1/_3$ cup SPLENDA® Granular (75 mL)

Yield: 8 servings
1 serving
250.9 calories
8.4 g protein
22.0 g fat
5.2 g carbs

In 2-quart (2 L) casserole dish, layer slices of Mini Sour Cream Pound Cake, page 44.

In large bowl, whisk eggs. Whisk in Da Vinci® Sugar Free Dulce De Leche Syrup, whipping cream and SPLENDA® Granular. Pour over cake slices. Bake in 350°F (180°C) oven 45 minutes, or until top of custard looks set. Allow to cool 10 minutes and serve with a dollop Crème Fraiche, page 67.

Variation: **Da Vinci® Alternative:** Substitute 2 tsp (10 mL) vanilla extract, replace Da Vinci® Sugar Free Syrup with $1^1/_2$ cups (375 mL) water and increase SPLENDA® Granular to $^2/_3$ cup (150 mL). (***6.3 g Carbs***)

Helpful Hints: Wrap remaining Mini Sour Cream Pound Cake in plastic wrap and foil and freeze for making this pudding again in the future, or for using in Peaches and Cream Trifle, page 24.

~~Low-Carb Dieting Tip~~
Calories do matter in my opinion. Smaller, shorter people will require fewer calories and it stands to reason that if one eats much more than the body requires, one cannot still expect to lose weight. It is true that a ketogenic diet is calorically wasteful, and that allows for eating more calories.

ORANGE CREAMSICLES

These were a hit!

$^1/_3$ cup Da Vinci® Sugar Free (75 mL)
 Orange Syrup
1 envelope unflavored gelatin
$^3/_4$ cup sour cream, OR yogurt (175 mL)
$^3/_4$ cup Da Vinci® Sugar Free (175 mL)
 Orange Syrup
$^1/_3$ cup SPLENDA® Granular (75 mL)
2 tbsp frozen orange juice from (25 mL)
 concentrate, undiluted

Yield: 8 popsicles
1 popsicle
46.8 calories
1.5 g protein
3.0 g fat
3.6 g carbs

In cereal bowl, combine $^1/_3$ cup (75 mL) Da Vinci® Sugar Free Orange Syrup and gelatin. Nuke 45 seconds in microwave oven. Set aside. In medium bowl, combine sour cream or plain yogurt, $^3/_4$ cup (175 mL) Da Vinci® Sugar Free Orange Syrup, SPLENDA® Granular and orange juice concentrate. Whisk in gelatin mixture. Pour into Popsicle molds. Freeze.

Variations: **Strawberry Orange Creamsicles:** Substitute Da Vinci® Sugar Free Strawberry Syrup. (*3.6 g Carbs*)

Raspberry Pineapple Creamsicles: Substitute Da Vinci® Sugar Free Raspberry Syrup and frozen pineapple juice from concentrate, undiluted. (*3.9 g Carbs*)

Da Vinci® Alternative: Replace syrup with water and use 1 envelope orange sugar free Kool-Aid® (or to taste). Use 8 SPLENDA® packets to sweeten. (*3.8 g Carbs*) and without orange juice concentrate: (*2.1 g Carbs*).

~~Low-Carb Dieting Tip~~
Counting calories is usually not necessary as a low-carb diet will naturally curb hunger and intake will be less, however, on a Fat Fast, it is imperative to count calories for success.

MANDARIN ORANGE JELLY

Cool and light for a hot day.

1 $^1/_2$ envelopes gelatin
2 tbsp cold water (25 mL)
1 cup boiling water (250 mL)
$^3/_4$ cup Da Vinci® Sugar Free (175 mL)
  Orange Syrup
1 $^1/_4$ cups cold water (300 mL)
4 SPLENDA® packets
1 cup canned mandarin orange (250 mL)
  segments

Yield: 4 servings
1 serving
38.4 calories
3.3 g protein
0.1 g fat
6.3 g carbs

In small bowl, add gelatin to cold water to soften. Pour boiling water over and stir to dissolve gelatin. Add Da Vinci® Sugar Free Orange Syrup, cold water and SPLENDA®; stir.

As jelly begins to set in refrigerator, fold in mandarin orange segments. Chill until fully set before serving. Serve with Delicious Pouring Custard, page 138, *Splendid Low-Carbing* or with a dollop Crème Fraiche, page 67.

Variations: **Vanilla Peach Jelly:** Substitute Da Vinci® Sugar Free Vanilla Syrup and 1 cup (250 mL) canned, sliced peaches, chopped. (*4.3 g Carbs*)

Mandarin Orange Peach Jelly: Substitute 1 cup (250 mL) canned, sliced peaches, chopped. (*4.3 g Carbs*)

Strawberry Jelly: Substitute Da Vinci® Sugar Free Strawberry Syrup and 1 cup (250 mL) sliced, fresh strawberries. (*3.0 g Carbs*)

Raspberry Jelly: Substitute Da Vinci® Sugar Free Raspberry Syrup and fresh raspberries. (*3.1 g Carbs*)

Bumble Berry Jelly: Substitute Da Vinci® Sugar Free Raspberry or Strawberry Syrup and fresh mixed berries. (*3.7 g Carbs*)

Da Vinci® Alternative: Use water and 1 or 1 $^1/_2$ envelopes sugarless Kool-Aid®. Increase sweetener to taste.

INSTANT STRAWBERRY FROZEN YOGURT

Instant dessert for anytime. This is a soft serve frozen yogurt.

2 cups frozen strawberries, (500 mL)
  (unsweetened)
1 cup plain yogurt (250 mL)
5 SPLENDA® packets

Yield: 2 cups (500 mL)
$^1/_2$ cup (125 mL) per serving
74.0 calories
2.9 g protein
2.1 g fat
7.5 g carbs

In colander, rinse strawberries (if necessary) very briefly under running cold water to remove any ice crystals. In food processor with sharp blade or in blender, process strawberries on slowest speed until coarsely chopped. Add yogurt and SPLENDA®. Process until smooth. Serve immediately or freeze until a little harder.

Variation: **Instant Peach Frozen Yogurt:** Use frozen, unsweetened peach slices or canned sliced peaches, drained and frozen. (*8.8 g Carbs*)

SNOW PUDDING

A lemony light gelatin pudding.

1 envelope gelatin
$^1/_4$ cup cold water (50 mL)
1 cup boiling water (250 mL)
6 SPLENDA® packets
$^1/_4$ cup lemon juice (50 mL)
2 tsp finely grated lemon peel (10 mL)
$1^1/_4$ cups Crème Fraiche, (300 mL)
  page 67

Yield: 4 servings
1 serving
149.2 calories
2.8 g protein
13.1 g fat
5.9 g carbs

In medium bowl, soak gelatin in cold water, then dissolve it in the boiling water. Stir in SPLENDA®, lemon juice and lemon peel. Chill until almost set.

Beat gelatin mixture with wire whisk 30 seconds until light and spongy. Fold in Crème Fraiche, page 67. Pour into 4-cup (1 L) pudding mold. Serve with Delicious Pouring Custard, page 138, *Splendid Low-Carbing*, if desired.

INSTANT FRUITY ICE CREAM

Tastes real fruity – very much like ice cream, just more fruity.

Strawberry Ice Cream:
2 cups frozen strawberries, (500 mL)
(unsweetened)
$^3/_4$ cup whipping cream (175 mL)
$^1/_2$ cup SPLENDA® Granular (125 mL)

Yield: 2$^1/_2$ cups (625 mL)
$^1/_2$ cup (125 mL) per serving
138.7 calories
1.0 g protein
11.6 g fat
7.7 g carbs

In colander, rinse strawberries very briefly under running cold water to remove any ice crystals. If there are no ice crystals, skip this step. In food processor with sharp blade or in blender, using slow speed, process strawberries until coarsely chopped. Use slow speed on food processor. Add whipping cream and SPLENDA® Granular. Process, increasing speed gradually until ice cream is smooth. Serve immediately. Freeze leftovers in sealed, plastic container. Microwave briefly and enjoy again.

Variation: **Peach Ice Cream:** Use one, 18 fl oz (796 mL) can peach slices in juice or water, drained well. Freeze peaches. Use when frozen as in recipe above. Use 5 SPLENDA® packets instead of SPLENDA® Granular to reduce carbs. *Yield:* 3 cups (750 mL), $^1/_2$ cup (125 mL) per serving. (*8.7 g Carbs*)

Helpful Hints: The strawberry ice cream is really fantastic served with thawed frozen, unsweetened strawberries, sweetened with SPLENDA® Granular. Pour Chocolate Sauce, page 70 or 71 over each serving, or melt a sugar free chocolate bar and stir in a little shortening (non-hydrogenated) or butter to use as a topping.

~~Low-Carb Dieting Tip~~
Binging on high-carb foods will set back weight loss for a few days at least.

RICH MAN'S CARAMEL CUSTARD

A rich, thick, smooth and sweet custard. My favorite!

2 cups SPLENDA® Granular (500 mL)
1 cup half-and-half cream (250 mL)
$^1/_2$ cup water (125 mL)
10 egg yolks
1 $^1/_8$ cups Condensed Milk*, (275 mL)
  page 68 (instead of water, use
  Da Vinci® Sugar Free Caramel Syrup)
1 tsp vanilla extract (5 mL)

Yield: 12/16 servings
1 serving
165.4/124.0 calories
5.9 g/4.4 g protein
11.7 g/8.8 g fat
8.7 g/6.5 g carbs

Caramel Sauce:
$^1/_4$ cup SPLENDA® Granular (50 mL)
2 tbsp Da Vinci® Sugar Free Caramel Syrup (25 mL)
2 tbsp water (25 mL)
$^1/_8$ tsp Thickening Agent (0.5 mL)
$^1/_8$ tsp maple extract (0.5 mL)

In large bowl, combine SPLENDA® Granular, half-and-half cream and water. Stir in egg yolks (do not beat). Add Condensed Milk, page 68; stir until everything is well incorporated. Lastly add vanilla extract. Strain custard, if desired.

Caramel Sauce: In small saucepan, combine SPLENDA® Granular, Da Vinci® Sugar Free Caramel Syrup, water and Thickening Agent. Bring to boil. Sieve and stir in maple extract. Divide sauce between two 9 x 5 x 3-inch (2 L) loaf pans (or 3 mini loaf pans), sprayed with nonstick cooking spray.

Pour custard into loaf pans over Caramel Sauce. Place loaf pans in larger pan and pour water in it, reaching $^1/_4$ way up the pans. Bake in 375°F (190°C) oven 25 to 30 minutes, or until cake tester or toothpick inserted in center comes out clean. Cool before serving. This custard may also be served chilled.

Helpful Hints: *Use only 2 tbsp (25 mL) melted butter in Condensed Milk, page 68. I was unsuccessful at unmolding these custards with my old, no longer nonstick pans. The trick is to wait until the custard has cooled completely, before inverting onto serving plates. Perhaps it would have been easier had I lined the loaf pans with wax paper on the bottom. It's easier, though, to dish up each serving onto a pretty serving plate.

VANILLA ICE CREAM

*Really lovely ice cream without eggs and made using Low-Carb Condensed Milk,
page 68. One of my best ice creams!*

Low-Carb Condensed Milk,
  Page 68 (use melted butter)
2 cups half-and-half cream (500 mL)
1 tbsp vanilla extract (15 mL)

> ***Yield:*** 4 cups (1 L)
> $^1/_2$ cup (125 mL) per serving
> 223.2 calories
> 6.3 g protein
> 18.6 g fat
> ***7.4 g carbs***

Prepare Low-Carb Condensed Milk, page 68 (make sure to use melted butter to prevent small lumps of butter forming in your ice cream); pour into large bowl. Stir in cream and vanilla extract; whisk until well combined. Refrigerate until chilled. Freeze in ice cream maker as manufacturer directs.

Variations: **Chocolate Ice Cream:** Add $^1/_4$ cup (50 mL) Dutch cocoa to blender along with half-and-half cream. Omit vanilla extract, OR add only 1 tsp (5 mL). (***7.5 g Carbs***)

Chocolate Mint Ice Cream: As for Chocolate Ice Cream, however, omit vanilla extract and use $^1/_2$ tsp (2 mL) mint and peppermint extract. (***7.5 g Carbs***)

Cappuccino Ice Cream: Dissolve 2 tsp (10 mL) instant coffee crystals in blender along with condensed milk and cream. Omit vanilla extract. (***7.3 g Carbs***)

Toasted Coconut Ice Cream: Use Low-Carb Condensed milk, page 68 and one 13.5 fl. oz (398 mL) can coconut milk, $^1/_4$ cup (50 mL) half-and-half cream and $^1/_4$ cup (50 mL) toasted coconut, 3 tbsp (45 mL) Da Vinci® Sugar Free Coconut Syrup and 2 SPLENDA® packets. (Toast coconut in dry, nonstick skillet.) (***7.1 g Carbs***)

Fruity Ice Creams: Use 1 cup (250 mL) fruit of choice, chopped or mashed.

Helpful Hints: Using whipping cream, one can shave off 1 gram carbohydrate, which doesn't seem worth it to me, in light of the fact that the calories go up by 100. However, for about the same calories, use 1 cup (250 mL) whipping cream and 1 cup (250 mL) water to shave off almost 2 g carbohydrate at ***5.6 g Carbs***. I like the recipe above, however, this would be a good alternative for those of you who must remain under 20 or 30 grams of carbohydrate per day.

PIES

SNOW-CAPPED PUMPKIN PIE

I'm not a huge fan of pumpkin pie, however, my son Jonathan, almost single-handedly polished off this pie.

1 Single Piecrust, page 42
Filling:
15 oz canned pumpkin (450 g)
10 SPLENDA® packets
$1^1/_2$ tsp pumpkin pie spice (7 mL)
$^1/_8$ tsp salt (0.5 mL)
2 eggs, slightly beaten with fork
$^3/_4$ cup half-and-half cream (175 mL)
1 cup Crème Fraiche, page 67 (250 mL)

Yield: 10 servings
1 serving
192.6 calories
8.4 g protein
14.5 g fat
7.3 g carbs

Single Piecrust: Prepare Single Piecrust, page 42, with straight edge in deep 9-inch (23 cm) glass baking dish as described, however, do not bake.

Filling: In medium bowl, combine pumpkin, SPLENDA®, pumpkin pie spice, salt and eggs. Whisk lightly. Gradually add half-and-half cream, while whisking. Pour over prepared crust. Place pie in oven and cover lightly with foil tent (do not allow foil to touch filling – see Helpful Hints, # 10, page 5). Bake in 375°F (190°C) oven 50 minutes, or until a cake tester inserted near center comes out clean.

Let cool on wire rack. When it reaches room temperature, cover (without touching pie) and refrigerate. Before serving, spread Crème Fraiche gently over surface of the pie.

~~Low-Carb Dieting Tip~~
Significantly restricting carbohydrates curbs hunger and makes it easier to eat less and thus lose weight.

STRAWBERRY RHUBARB CRUMBLE TART

Now we can occasionally enjoy old favorites again.

1 unbaked Single Piecrust, page 42
Filling:
10 oz frozen strawberries, (300 g)
  unsweetened
10 oz frozen rhubarb, (300 g)
  unsweetened
1 cup SPLENDA® Granular (250 mL)
2 tbsp water (25 mL)
1 tsp Thickening Agent, page 66 (5 mL)
1 tsp vanilla extract (5 mL)
Crumble Topping:
$^1/_2$ cup ground almonds, lightly toasted (125 mL)
$^1/_4$ cup vanilla whey protein (50 mL)
$^1/_4$ cup butter, melted (50 mL)

Yield: 10 servings
1 serving
204.0 calories
8.8 g protein
15.2 g fat
7.5 g carbs

Single Piecrust: Prepare piecrust as directed on page 42, however, do not bake.

Filling: In medium saucepan, place strawberries, rhubarb, SPLENDA® Granular, water and Thickening Agent, page 66. Stir well. Bring to boil over medium heat, stirring occasionally, until sauce has thickened. Remove from heat; stir in vanilla extract. Let cool slightly; pour into prepared piecrust. Sprinkle Crumble Topping over fruit. Place pie in oven and cover lightly with foil. Bake in 375°F (190°C) oven 25 to 30 minutes, or until fruit is hot and crust is golden brown. Serve with a dollop Crème Fraiche, page 67, if desired.

Crumble Topping: In small bowl, combine ground almonds, vanilla whey protein and melted butter.

Variation: Strawberry Raspberry Crumble Tart: Substitute frozen unsweetened raspberries for frozen rhubarb. (**8.4 g Carbs**)

~~Low-Carb Dieting Tip~~
Reduced immunity occurs, as one gets older. Take antioxidants such as selenium and vitamins E and C. These are particularly important for someone with an autoimmune disease such as Hashimoto's Thyroiditis.

GLAZED BLUEBERRY CHEESE PIE

A slice of this pie looks beautiful on a plate and tastes exquisite.

Single Piecrust, page 42
Filling:
1 cup ricotta cheese (250 mL)
5 oz regular cream cheese (150 g)
$^1/_2$ cup SPLENDA® Granular (125 mL)
2 tsp lemon juice (10 mL)
Blueberry Topping:
1$^3/_4$ cups frozen blueberries, (425 mL)
  (unsweetened)
$^1/_2$ cup water (125 mL)
$^1/_4$ cup SPLENDA® Granular (50 mL)
$^3/_4$ tsp Thickening Agent, page 66 (3 mL)

Yield: 10 servings
1 serving
195.5 calories
9.3 g protein
14.3 g fat
7.3 g carbs

Single Piecrust: Follow directions on page 42. Bake as directed.

Filling: In food processor with sharp blade, blender or in bowl with electric mixer, process ricotta cheese until smooth. Add cream cheese, SPLENDA® Granular and lemon juice; process until smooth. Spread evenly over baked crust. Chill until firm.

Blueberry Topping: In saucepan, combine blueberries, water, SPLENDA® Granular and Thickening Agent, page 66. Bring to boil and cook until blueberry sauce thickens. Allow to cool slightly. Pour topping over chilled cheese layer, leaving outer edge bare. Refrigerate pie. Later garnish with Crème Fraiche, page 67 around outer edge of pie, if desired.

Variations: **Glazed Raspberry Cheese Pie:** Substitute frozen unsweetened raspberries. (*6.6 g Carbs*)

Glazed Strawberry Cheese Pie: Substitute frozen unsweetened strawberries. (*6.7 g Carbs*).

~~Low-Carb Dieting Tip~~
Exercise definitely helps weight loss and helps firm jiggly areas.

CHOCOLATE PECAN PIE

The texture of this pecan pie is fabulous. My husband thought it was great.

Single Piecrust, page 42
Filling:
1 recipe Condensed Milk*, page 68
  (omit SPLENDA® Granular and
  use 32 SPLENDA® packets)*
1 cup sugarless chocolate chips, (250 mL)
  (sweetened)
2 eggs, fork beaten
$^1/_4$ tsp salt (1 mL)
$1^1/_2$ cups pecan halves (375 mL)

Yield: 12/16 servings
1 serving
359.1/269.3 calories
10.4/7.8 g protein
28.4/21.3 g fat
9.4/7.1 g carbs

Single Piecrust: Prepare as directed on page 42 in a shallow 9-inch (23 cm) glass pie dish. Do not bake.

Filling: *Prepare Condensed Milk, page 68 either in blender or in food processor (with sharp blade). Use 32 SPLENDA® packets for sweetening. Also use Da Vinci® Sugar Free French Vanilla or Vanilla Syrup instead of water.

In double boiler, combine Condensed Milk, page 68 and chocolate chips. Melt over medium heat. Remove from heat. Stir in eggs, salt and pecan halves. Pour over prepared crust. Bake in 350°F (180°C) oven on bottom shelf 30 minutes. Cover with foil after 20 minutes, to protect the crust from becoming too brown. Chill pie. It is preferable to serve the pie cold.

Helpful Hints: This pecan pie, just as with all regular pecan pies, is truly decadent and the calories are high, therefore the servings are smaller. It is actually quite easy to cut slivers, if that's all you want at a sitting.

~~Low-Carb Dieting Tip~~
Eating eggs for breakfast staves off hunger for hours.

KEY LIME PIE

A dessert to be enjoyed any time of year. This dessert probably tastes a little different to the classic dessert, however, it is good.

Single Piecrust, page 42
Filling:
3 eggs
1 recipe Condensed Milk,* page 68
$^1/_2$ cup fresh Key lime juice (125 mL)
3 tbsp water (45 mL)
few drops green food coloring,
  (optional)
1 cup Crème Fraiche, page 67 (250 mL)

Yield: 10 servings
1 serving
279.7 calories
11.6 g protein
23.1 g fat
7.2 g carbs

Single Piecrust: Prepare crust on page 42. Bake as directed 5 minutes.

Filling: In medium bowl, whisk eggs. Whisk in condensed milk. Add lime juice, water and, if desired, green food coloring. Combine well. Pour over prepared crust.

Place in 350°F (180°C) oven. Cover pie lightly with foil tent, without touching filling. Bake 35 minutes, or until set. Cool on wire rack to room temperature.

Cover surface of pie with Crème Fraiche, page 67. Serve chilled.

Helpful Hints: Key limes are small and about half the size of the Persian limes. If Key limes are not available, substitute half lemon juice and half Persian lime juice.

*Use Da Vinci® Sugar Free Vanilla Syrup in Condensed Milk, page 68 or add a few packets sweetener.

~~Low-Carb Dieting Tip~~
Eating eggs is supposed to help firm jiggly areas on the body.

STRAWBERRY FROZEN ICE CREAM PIE

Jonathan loved this pie!

Crust:
$^1/_2$ cup Low-Carb Bake Mix, (125 mL)
  page 22
$^1/_2$ cup ground almonds (125 mL)
$^1/_4$ cup butter, melted (50 mL)
1 SPLENDA® packet

Filling:
10 oz frozen strawberries, (300 g)
  (unsweetened), thawed and drained
$^1/_4$ cup SPLENDA® Granular (50 mL)
3 cups Vanilla Ice Cream, page 31, (750 mL)
  (freshly made)

Yield: 10 servings
1 serving
246.5 calories
7.3 g protein
20.5 g fat
8.1 g carbs

Crust: In small bowl, combine Low-Carb Bake Mix, page 22, ground almonds, butter and SPLENDA®. Spread in 9-inch (23 cm) glass baking dish. Cover with plastic wrap. Press crust out evenly on bottom of dish; remove wrap. Bake in 350°F (180°C) oven 10 minutes.

Filling: In medium bowl, combine thawed, drained strawberries and SPLENDA® Granular. Stir in Vanilla Ice Cream, page 31. Pour over crust. Freeze.

To serve, thaw 20 minutes to half an hour or thaw briefly in microwave oven.

~~Low-Carb Dieting Tip~~
The beauty of slower weight loss is that the body has time to accommodate the many changes that occur.

ALMOND BUTTER CHIP PIE

A rich, decadent-tasting pie. Divide into 12 servings, as for a cheesecake baked in a pie dish. It's a cross between a cheesecake and a pie in ingredients; however, its fudgy consistency is unlike a cheesecake.

Almond Chocolate Crust:
1 cup ground almonds (250 mL)
1 SPLENDA® packet
1 egg white
2 tbsp sugarless chocolate chips, (25 mL)
  melted (usually maltitol-sweetened)

Filling:
8 oz regular cream cheese, (250 g)
  softened
$^3/_4$ cup Crème Fraiche, page 67 (175 mL)
$^3/_4$ cup almond butter (175 mL)
$^1/_3$ cup Confectioner's Sugar, (75 mL)
  Substitute, page 65
5 SPLENDA® packets
$^1/_2$ tsp vanilla extract (2 mL)
$^1/_8$ tsp salt (0.5 mL)
$^3/_4$ cup sugarless chocolate chips, (175 mL)
  (usually maltitol-sweetened)

Yield: 12 servings
1 serving
292.3 calories
8.0 g protein
26.9 g fat
6.6 g carbs

Almond Chocolate Crust: In small bowl, combine ground almonds, SPLENDA® packet and egg white. Stir in chocolate. Spread in 9-inch (23 cm) glass pie dish. Cover with plastic wrap. Press crust out evenly; remove wrap. Bake in 350°F (180°C) oven 10 minutes.

Filling: In food processor with sharp blade, blender or in bowl with electric mixer, process cream cheese until smooth. Add Crème Fraiche, page 67, almond butter, Confectioner's Sugar Substitute, page 65, SPLENDA®, vanilla extract and salt. Process until smooth. Stir in chocolate chips. Spread over hot, baked crust. Place in refrigerator immediately (on something heatproof).

Variation: Peanut Butter Chip Pie: Use sugar free and salt free peanut butter instead. (*6.2 g Carbs*)

~~Low-Carb Dieting Tip~~
For people who think low-carb dieting is dangerous: ask them what is so dangerous about eliminating refined white flour and sugar from the diet?

STRAWBERRY CREAM PIE
Strawberries and cream in a pie shell!

Refrigerator Piecrust, page 43
Filling:
4 cups frozen strawberries (1 L)
  (unsweetened)
6 SPLENDA® packets
$^1/_8$ tsp salt (0.5 mL)
2 tbsp water (25 mL)
1 tbsp unflavored gelatin (15 mL)
Topping:
$1^1/_4$ cups Crème Fraiche, page 67 (300 mL)
few fresh strawberries, sliced, for garnish,
  (optional)

Yield: 10 servings
1 serving
221.6 calories
6.2 g protein
18.9 g fat
7.1 g carbs

Refrigerator Piecrust: Follow instructions on page 43 and bake as directed.

Filling: In medium saucepan, combine strawberries, SPLENDA® and salt. In cereal bowl, pour water and stir in gelatin. Microwave 45 seconds; stir. Add to strawberries. Bring strawberry mixture to boil. Set aside to cool. Pour into container and refrigerate until thickening slightly.

Pour into prepared pie shell. When strawberry filling has set, spread with Crème Fraiche, page 67 over top.

Topping: Prepare Crème Fraiche, page 67. Garnish pie with a few slices of fresh strawberries, if desired.

Helpful Hint: Semi-thaw strawberries and slice large ones in half.

~~Low-Carb Dieting Tip~~
Patience is a virtue. The weight did not come on overnight, nor will it fall off overnight, however, stick with it and one morning in the future, you will wake up a skinnier version of you!

BUTTERSCOTCH CREAM PIE
Old fashioned cream pie. Daniel likes this pie.

Almond Crust:
1 cup ground almonds (250 mL)
1 SPLENDA® packet
1 egg white
Filling:
8 oz regular cream cheese (250 g)
1 cup whipping cream (250 mL)
1 cup SPLENDA® Granular (250 mL)
1 package diet butterscotch pudding (40 g)
1 cup Crème Fraiche, page 67 (250 mL)

Yield: 10 servings
1 serving
281.2 calories
6.0 g protein
25.2 g fat
8.3 g carbs

Almond Crust: In small bowl, combine ground almonds, SPLENDA® and egg white. Spread in 9-inch (23 cm) glass pie dish. Cover with plastic wrap. Press crust out evenly; remove wrap. Bake in 350°F (180°C) oven 10 minutes. Cover with foil and bake another 5 minutes.

Filling: In food processor with sharp blade, blender or in bowl with electric mixer, process cream cheese until smooth. Add whipping cream, SPLENDA® Granular and butterscotch pudding; process until smooth. Add Crème Fraiche, page 67; process.

Carefully spread filling over cooled crust. Refrigerate pie.

Variations: Lemon Cream Pie: Use diet lemon pudding.

Chocolate Cream Pie: Use diet chocolate pudding.

Vanilla Cream Pie: Use diet vanilla pudding.

Helpful Hints: Cream pies go well with banana. On maintenance, when an extra 3 g carbs does not matter quite as much, slice a banana thinly, dip in lemon juice and layer the slices over the crust before adding the filling.

~~Low-Carb Dieting Tip~~
Choose low-glycemic foods for more stable blood-sugar.

CHOCOLATE MINT ICE CREAM PIE

The texture reminds one of a fudgsicle. Jonathan loved this!

Crust:
$^1/_2$ cup Low-Carb Bake Mix, (125 mL)
  page 22
$^1/_2$ cup ground almonds (125 mL)
$^1/_4$ cup butter, melted (50 mL)
1 SPLENDA® packet
Filling:
4 cups Chocolate Mint Ice Cream, (1 L)
  page 31 (freshly made)

Yield: 10 servings
1 serving
239.0 calories
8.8 g protein
19.7 g fat
7.0 g carbs

Crust: In small bowl, combine Low-Carb Bake Mix, page 22, ground almonds, butter and SPLENDA®. Spread in 9-inch (23 cm) glass baking dish. Cover with plastic wrap. Press crust out evenly on bottom of dish; remove wrap. Bake in 350°F (180°C) oven 10 minutes.

Filling: Spread ice cream carefully over cooled crust. Freeze. To serve, thaw 20 minutes to half an hour or thaw briefly in microwave oven.

GRAHAM CRACKER-LIKE CRUST

Very similar to a substantial graham cracker crust, perhaps just not as sweet.
Add extra sweetener, if desired.

$^2/_3$ cup Low-Carb Bake Mix, (150 mL)
  page 22
$^2/_3$ cup ground almonds (150 mL)
$^1/_3$ cup butter, melted (75 mL)
2 SPLENDA® packets

Yield: 10 servings
1 serving
128.9 calories
4.4 g protein
11.9 g fat
1.4 g carbs

In medium bowl, combine Low-Carb Bake Mix, page 22, ground almonds, butter and SPLENDA®. Press into 9-inch (23 cm) glass pie dish. Bake in 350°F (180°C) oven 10 minutes, or until turning light brown.

Helpful Hint: See page 86 for a realistic Graham Cracker-like crust for a 9 x 13-inch (23 x 33 cm) baking dish.

SINGLE PIECRUST

This is a lower carb and more substantial crust that tastes great.

1 1/8 cups Low-Carb Bake Mix, (275 mL)
  page 22
3 oz cream cheese, softened (90 g)
1 tbsp SPLENDA® Granular (15 mL)
1 tbsp butter, softened (15 mL)
1/4 tsp baking soda (1 mL)
1/8 tsp salt (0.5 mL)

Yield: 10 servings	
1 serving	
94.4 calories	
5.7 g protein	
7.3 g fat	
1.6 g carbs	

In food processor or in bowl with electric mixer, process Low-Carb Bake Mix, page 22, cream cheese, SPLENDA® Granular, butter, baking soda and salt until mixed. Form a ball with dough using your hands. Chill dough about 1 hour.

Roll dough out between two sheets of wax paper to fit shallow 9-inch (23 cm) glass pie dish with a flat border (do not roll out too thin). Remove top sheet of wax paper. Pick up sheet with dough and invert over pie dish. Use flat dinner knife to carefully ease dough off wax paper. Use small rolling pin or small cylindrical object in pie dish, if necessary, to further roll dough. Patch dough where required.

Press dough onto pie dish border, cut to size and patch where necessary. Make an attractive edging by pressing dough with tines of fork and leaving spaces in between. Bake in 350°F (180°C) oven 10 minutes, or until golden brown. This crust browns extremely quickly; therefore, if baking again with filling, it's best to bake only 5 minutes before adding filling and baking. Cover pie lightly with foil tent (See Helpful Hints, #10, page 5) from beginning of baking to end, otherwise crust becomes too dark. It will still be edible, but it's best to aim for a golden brown color.

Helpful Hints: If using a deep 9-inch (23 cm) pie dish for more substantial fillings, press dough up sides only (straight edge). Push down slightly from edge onto dough with thumbs and this will make a slightly thicker border for the crust. It is possible to skip chilling the dough, however, it is easier to handle when chilled.

~~Low-Carb Dieting Tip~~
Fat causes virtually no blood-sugar elevations and protein cause very little.

REFRIGERATOR PIECRUSTS

Lovely low-carb piecrusts for pies that will need to be refrigerated. Coconut oil has been touted as helpful for losing weight.

$2^1/_4$ cups Low-Carb Bake Mix, (550 mL) page 22
$^1/_2$ tsp salt (2 mL)
$^1/_2$ cup coconut oil (125 mL)
$^1/_4$ cup unsalted butter (50 mL)
1 tbsp cold water (15 mL)

Yield: 2 crusts, 20 servings
1 serving
122.9 calories
4.9 g protein
11.3 g fat
1.1 g carbs

In large bowl, combine Low-Carb Bake Mix, page 22 and salt. Cut in coconut oil and butter with pastry knife or rub in using hands. Sprinkle water over dough and mix in well. Weigh dough and divide into equal portions by weight. Press into bottom of 2, 9-inch (23 cm) glass pie dishes and about 1-inch (2.5 cm) up to edge of pie dishes. Keep it a straight edge, no crimping etc. of the dough, as it does not lend itself to that.

Bake in 350°F (180°C) oven 10 minutes, or until turning light brown. Allow to cool slightly.

Helpful Hints: Wrap dough that will not be used right away in plastic wrap and foil and place in refrigerator. To reuse, microwave 30 seconds. This piecrust will freeze well for at least one month. Thaw before using.

These crusts may be used in unbaked form. Add filling and bake as directed. Do watch as these crusts brown very easily. Cover with foil loosely as soon as crust is dark enough (usually check after 10 minutes). If perchance you over bake the crust, it will still taste fine, but is better if not overcooked.

The baked, hot crust is quite unstable and crumbly, however, it sets up beautifully in the refrigerator and can remain at room temperature for an hour or two after removing from the refrigerator.

~~Low-Carb Dieting Tip~~
Too much protein at a sitting will be converted by the body into glucose.

CAKES

MINI SOUR CREAM POUND CAKES

These are fairly plain though lovely served with apricot fruit spread. It is useful to use in a trifle, page 24 or cake pudding, page 25.

$^1/_2$ cup butter, softened (125 mL)
3 eggs
1 cup SPLENDA® Granular (250 mL)
1 tsp vanilla extract (5 mL)
$1^3/_4$ cups Low-Carb Bake Mix, (425 mL)
 page 22
$^1/_2$ tsp baking powder (2 mL)
$^1/_4$ tsp baking soda (1 mL)
$^1/_2$ cup sour cream (125 mL)

Yield: 24 mini slices
1 mini slice
91.1 calories
4.1 g protein
7.4 g fat
2.0 g carbs

In food processor or mixing bowl with an electric mixer, process butter until smooth. While processing add eggs one at a time. Add SPLENDA® Granular and vanilla extract; process.

In medium bowl, combine Low-Carb Bake Mix, page 22, baking powder and baking soda.

Alternately add dry ingredients and sour cream to egg mixture, while processing. Process each time only until combined. Pour batter into 2 greased nonstick $5^3/_4$ x $3^1/_4$ x $2^1/_4$ inch (15 x 8 x 6 cm) mini loaf pans. Bake in 325°F (160°C) oven 40 minutes, or until turning light brown on top and a wooden toothpick inserted near center comes out clean. Cool on wire rack 10 minutes and remove loaves.

~~Low-Carb Dieting Tip~~
Everyone is different! Read about all the different low-carb diets and find one that suits your tastes and lifestyle.

CHOCOLATE SWEETHEART CAKE

This beautiful, layered cake rises very high and tastes like the real thing.

$2^1/_2$ cups Low-Carb Bake Mix, (625 mL) page 22
$1^1/_4$ cups SPLENDA® Granular (300 mL)
$^1/_4$ cup cocoa (50 mL)
$^1/_4$ cup maltitol crystals* (50 mL)
2 tsp baking soda (10 mL)
$^1/_2$ tsp salt (2 mL)
$^3/_4$ cup sour cream (175 mL)
$^2/_3$ cup light-tasting olive oil (150 mL)
3 eggs
$^1/_4$ cup Da Vinci® Sugar Free (50 mL) Chocolate, OR any low-carb pancake syrup
2 tsp vanilla extract (10 mL)
Chocolate Frosting, page 70 or 71

> **Yield:** 12/16 servings
> 1 serving
> 373.0/279.8 calories
> 12.3/9.2 g protein
> 29.1/21.8 g fat
> **8.9/6.8 g carbs**

In large bowl with electric mixer or in food processor, combine Low-Carb Bake Mix, page 22, SPLENDA® Granular, cocoa, maltitol crystals, baking soda and salt. Stir to combine well. Add sour cream, olive oil, eggs, Da Vinci® Sugar Free Syrup of choice and vanilla extract. Beat on low speed until well combined.

Spread batter evenly in two greased and "floured" (see Helpful Hints, #11, page 6) 7-inch (18 cm) heart-shaped nonstick cake pans or 2, 8-inch (20 cm) cake pans. Bake in 350°F (180°C) oven 25 to 30 minutes. Test cake with knife in center of one cake after 25 minutes and check every 2 minutes thereafter, until knife comes out clean. Cool 10 minutes in pans on wire rack. Carefully run a knife around edges and lift underneath with a spatula. Invert cakes onto cake rack and cool. Turn one layer of cake on its topside, so that the two flat sides meet in the middle. Frost with **Chocolate Frosting, page 70 or 71**. If desired, place a heart-shaped patch of Crème Fraiche, page 67 on top of cake over chocolate frosting and garnish with 1 or 2 red candied cherries cut into tiny pieces for color. Sprinkle with unsweetened grated chocolate. If desired, in center, spread Crème Fraiche, page 67, whipped cream or strawberry fruit spread or a mixture of the two. Garnish sides of the cake with pecan halves, if desired.

Helpful Hints: *I have made this cake using $1^1/_2$ cups (375 mL) SPLENDA® Granular, however it was not sweet enough, hence the reason for using maltitol crystals. On the can, it says to use 0 g net carbs per tsp (5 mL), however, I decided to count half of the 4 g carbs, just to be on the safe side. If you cannot tolerate maltitol, try using 1 cup (250 mL) SPLENDA® Granular plus 24 SPLENDA® packets or substitute another sweetener of your choice for maltitol.

CARROT CAKE

We loved this cake – it sure doesn't taste low-carb! Unfortunately, we ate too much of it in one sitting. It was such a treat.

1 $^1/_2$ cups Vital Oat Ultimate (375 mL)
  Bake Mix, page 20
1 cup SPLENDA® Granular (250 mL)
1 tsp cinnamon (5 mL)
1 tsp baking powder (5 mL)
$^1/_2$ tsp baking soda (2 mL)
$^1/_2$ cup grated zucchini (125 mL)
$^1/_2$ cup grated carrot (125 mL)
$^1/_3$ cup raisins, snipped in half (75 mL)
$^1/_2$ cup olive oil (125 mL)
2 eggs, fork beaten
1 tsp vanilla extract (5 mL)
1 tbsp olive oil (15 mL)
Cream Cheese Frosting:
4 oz light cream cheese, softened (125 g)
$^1/_3$ cup SPLENDA® Granular (75 mL)
2 tbsp unsalted butter, softened (25 mL)
1 tbsp whipping cream (15 mL)
1 tsp vanilla extract (5 mL)

Yield: 18 slices
1 slice with frosting
161.4 calories
4.1 g protein
13.1 g fat
6.5 g carbs

In large bowl, combine Vital Oat Ultimate Bake Mix, page 20, SPLENDA® Granular, cinnamon, baking powder and baking soda. Stir in zucchini, carrot and raisins. In medium bowl, pour $^1/_2$ cup (125 mL) olive oil. Add eggs and vanilla extract. Add to carrot cake mixture and stir until combined.

Line 9 x 5 x 3-inch (2 L) loaf pan with wax paper. Spray with nonstick cooking spray. Pour batter into pan. Sprinkle with 1 tbsp (15 mL) olive oil and stir in lightly. Bake in 375°F (190°C) oven 10 minutes, reduce heat to 350°F (180°C) and bake a further 20 minutes, or until cake tester comes out clean. Place loaf pan on wire rack and let loaf cool 10 minutes. Remove loaf and carefully remove wax paper. Frost loaf when completely cool.

Cream Cheese Frosting: In food processor with sharp blade or in blender, process cream cheese, SPLENDA® Granular, butter, whipping cream and vanilla extract until smooth.

LEMON TEA CAKE

Very simple to make this moist, lemon-flavored cake. The frosting is just enough to give the cake a tangy, lemon flavor and an attractive coating. However, if you prefer more frosting, go ahead and double up.

2 cups Low-Carb Bake Mix, (500 mL)
  page 22
1 cup SPLENDA® Granular (250 mL)
2 tsp baking powder (10 mL)
4 eggs
$^2/_3$ cup sour cream (150 mL)
$^1/_2$ cup olive oil (125 mL)
$^1/_4$ cup lemon juice (50 mL)
2 tbsp finely grated lemon peel (25 mL)

Yield: 10/12 servings
1 serving
270.3/225.2 calories
12.3/10.2 g protein
21.6/18.0 g fat
7.3/6.0 g carbs

Frosting:
$^1/_4$ cup Confectioner's Sugar Substititute, page 65 (50 mL)
2 tbsp lemon juice (25 mL)
1 tbsp water, OR lemon juice (15 mL)

In large bowl, combine Low-Carb Bake Mix, page 22, SPLENDA® Granular and baking powder. In medium bowl, whisk eggs with wire whisk. Whisk in sour cream, olive oil, lemon juice and lemon peel. Add to dry ingredients and mix well. Pour into 9-inch (23 cm) springform pan. Smooth out with back of spoon making sides higher than center.

Bake in 350°F (180°C) oven 30 minutes, or until cake tester inserted in center comes out clean. Frost warm cake.

Frosting: In small saucepan, combine Confectioner's Sugar Substitute, page 65, lemon juice and water, if using. Stir and heat just until beginning to bubble.

~~Low-Carb Dieting Tip~~
You are in control of what goes into your mouth. No one is force-feeding you. You also always have the right to politely refuse food offered that is not on plan.

GOLDEN FRUITCAKE

Do you miss traditional fruitcake? I'm not really a fan of fruitcake, however, I really enjoyed this lighter version. This fruitcake is quite moderate in carbs compared to the real thing.

$^1/_3$ cup dried apricots, chopped (75 mL)
$^1/_4$ cup seedless California raisins (50 mL)
$^1/_4$ cup chopped dates (50 mL)
$^1/_4$ cup slivered almonds, (50 mL)
  lightly toasted, chopped
1 tbsp lemon juice (15 mL)
2 tsp rum extract (10 mL)
1 tsp vanilla extract (5 mL)
1 tsp grated lemon peel (5 mL)
$1^3/_4$ cups Low-Carb Bake Mix, page 22 (425 mL)
$^3/_4$ cup SPLENDA® Granular (175 mL)
$^3/_4$ tsp baking soda (3 mL)
2 eggs, separated
$^1/_4$ cup butter, softened (50 mL)
$^1/_2$ cup yogurt (125 mL)

Yield: 10 slices per loaf
1 slice/without icing
130.7/106.4 calories
6.1/5.2 g protein
8.3/6.6 g fat
7.7/6.3 g carbs

Icing:
$^3/_4$ cup Confectioner's Sugar Substitute, page 65 (175 mL)
2 tbsp butter, melted (25 mL)
$^1/_4$ cup Da Vinci® Sugar Free French Vanilla Syrup, OR (50 mL)
  Low-Carb Pancake Syrup

In medium bowl, combine dried apricots, raisins, dates and almonds. Stir in lemon juice, rum extract, vanilla extract and lemon peel. Set aside. In another medium bowl, combine Low-Carb Bake Mix, page 22, SPLENDA® Granular and baking soda.

In food processor with whipping assembly, whip egg whites until stiff. In mixing bowl with electric mixer, beat egg yolks and butter together. To egg yolk mixture, add half dry ingredients, yogurt and remaining dry ingredients. Fold egg whites into batter and stir in fruit and nut mixture. Spread evenly in two greased nonstick $5^3/_4$ x $3^1/_4$ x $2^1/_4$ inch (15 x 8 x 6 cm) mini loaf pans. Bake in 300°F (150°C) oven 35 to 40 minutes, or until cake tester comes out clean. Let cool in pans on wire rack 10 minutes. Turn out and frost with Icing. Cover and store at room temperature for 2 days. Refrigerate thereafter.

Icing: In small bowl, whisk together Confectioner's Sugar Substitute, page 65, butter and Da Vinci® Sugar Free French Vanilla Syrup. Add extra syrup as needed.

APPLE CINNAMON COFFEE CAKE

Lovely, fragrant cake to serve with coffee or tea. Very quick and easy to throw together (provided you already have some bake mix made up), even when company pitches up on your doorstep unexpectedly. This cake will probably become a favorite.

$2^1/_4$ cups Low-Carb Bake Mix, (550 mL)
   page 22
$1^1/_2$ cups SPLENDA® Granular (375 mL)
1 tsp baking powder (5 mL)
1 tsp baking soda (5 mL)
1 tsp cinnamon (5 mL)
$^1/_2$ tsp salt (2 mL)
$^2/_3$ cup unsalted butter, softened (150 mL)
$^1/_2$ cup Da Vinci® Sugar Free (125 mL)
   Toasted Marshmallow, OR Vanilla, OR Cinnamon Syrup
$^1/_4$ cup whipping cream (50 mL)
2 apples, peeled, cored and diced
2 eggs
Topping:
$^1/_2$ cup SPLENDA® Granular (125 mL)
$^1/_2$ cup diced almonds, toasted (125 mL)
1 tsp cinnamon (5 mL)
$^1/_4$ tsp nutmeg, (optional) (1 mL)

Yield: 24 servings
1 serving
139.7 calories
5.4 g protein
11.0 g fat
5.0 g carbs

In large mixing bowl or in food processor, combine Low-Carb Bake Mix, page 22, SPLENDA® Granular, baking powder, baking soda, cinnamon, salt, butter, Da Vinci® Sugar Free Syrup of choice and whipping cream. Beat until combined.

Pour batter in greased 9 x 13-inch (23 x 33 cm) glass baking dish. Sprinkle diced apple over batter and distribute evenly, pressing apples into batter. Sprinkle topping over batter. Bake in 350°F (180°C) oven 20 minutes. Serve warm with Crème Fraiche, page 67.

Topping: In small bowl, combine SPLENDA® Granular, almonds, cinnamon and nutmeg.

Variation: **Da Vinci® Alternative:** Substitute water, 1 tsp (5 mL) vanilla extract and use $1^2/_3$ cups (400 mL) SPLENDA® Granular. (***5.2 g Carbs***)

Helpful Hints: Toast almonds in dry, nonstick skillet over medium heat, until turning brown. To reduce carbs, use only one apple. (***4.2 g Carbs***)

PECAN CHOCOLATE SWEETHEART CAKE

A beautiful, layered cake on Valentine's Day for your special sweetheart.

6 large eggs, separated and at
  room temperature
$^3/_4$ cup SPLENDA® Granular (175 mL)
$1^1/_2$ tsp vanilla extract (7 mL)
1 tsp rum extract (5 mL)
2 cups pecan halves, ground (500 mL)
Chocolate Frosting, page 70, OR 71
$^1/_2$ cup Crème Fraiche, page 67 (125 mL)

Yield: 12 servings
1 serving
289.3 calories
5.7 g protein
24.2 g fat
5.8 g carbs

In mixing bowl, beat egg yolks with all but 2 tbsp (25 mL) SPLENDA® Granular until thick and pale. Beat in vanilla and rum extracts. Stir in ground pecans.

In food processor, with whipping assembly, process egg whites until stiff peaks begin to form. Add SPLENDA® Granular; process. Fold $^1/_3$ of egg whites into pecan mixture and then fold in remaining egg whites. Spread batter in two greased 7-inch (18 cm) heart-shaped nonstick cake pans, making sides a little higher than center. Bake in 325°F (160°C) oven 20 minutes, or until turning brown.

Cool on wire rack in pans 10 minutes. Using a flat spatula, make sure that cake is not sticking anywhere along the sides or underneath. Invert. When completely cool, these cakes may be covered in plastic wrap and refrigerated a day or so, until time to decorate and frost.

Chocolate Frosting: Prepare as directed on page 70 or page 71.

Use Crème Fraiche, page 67 to frost middle of cake. Frost top and sides of cake with Chocolate Frosting, page 70 or 71. Sparsely sprinkle top of cake with chopped pecans, if desired.

Helpful Hints: Chocolate Fudge Frosting, page 88 may be used instead – just double up the recipe. (***6.7 g Carbs***)

~~Low-Carb Dieting Tip~~
Going on vacation? Pack your own low-carb treats and place them in a cooler.

GINGERBREAD

Serve this gingerbread with Caramel Sauce, page 69 or drizzle each serving with Icing, page 91.

1³/₄ cups Low-Carb Bake (425 mL)
  Mix, page 22
1 tsp baking powder (5 mL)
¹/₂ tsp baking soda (2 mL)
³/₄ tsp cinnamon (3 mL)
³/₄ tsp ginger (3 mL)
¹/₃ cup butter, softened (75 mL)
1 tbsp olive oil (15 mL)
1 egg
¹/₂ cup Molasses Substitute, page 71 (125 mL)
¹/₃ cup SPLENDA® Granular (75 mL)
¹/₄ cup water (50 mL)

Yield: 12 servings 1 serving 147.8 calories 6.9 g protein 11.8 g fat ***3.8 g carbs***

In medium bowl, combine Low-Carb Bake Mix, page 22, baking powder, baking soda, cinnamon and ginger. In food processor with sharp blade or in bowl with electric mixer, process butter and olive oil. Add egg, Molasses Substitute, page 71 and SPLENDA® Granular; process. Add dry ingredients alternately with water; process until combined.

Pour into greased 9-inch (23 cm) round cake pan, spreading cake batter slightly higher at circumference. Bake in 350°F (180°C) oven 25 minutes, or until cake tester comes out clean. Allow to cool slightly on wire rack in pan. Serve warm with Caramel Sauce, page 69 or drizzle each serving with Icing, page 19. Another option is to use Delicious Pouring Custard, page 138, *Splendid Low-Carbing.*

~~Low-Carb Dieting Tip~~
It takes doing something new 20 times for it to become a habit. This applies to exercise as well.

SPICY CHIFFON CAKE

A deliciously spiced cake with a thick, sticky toffee or condensed milk-like frosting. This lovely cake is one that my dear friend and mother figure in my life, Jeanne Lobsinger of Vernon, B.C., gave me. She used to make a higher carb version for birthdays for family and special friends.

2 cups Vital Oat Ultimate Bake (500 mL)
  Mix, page 20
1²/₃ cups Da Vinci® Sugar (400 mL)
1 tbsp baking powder (15 mL)
1 tsp cinnamon (5 mL)
¹/₂ tsp salt (2 mL)
¹/₂ tsp nutmeg (2 mL)
¹/₂ tsp allspice (2 mL)
¹/₂ tsp cloves (2 mL)
¹/₂ cup olive oil (125 mL)
7 unbeaten egg yolks
¹/₂ cup Da Vinci® Sugar Free Vanilla Syrup, OR (125 mL)
  water, 2 SPLENDA® packets and ¹/₂ tsp (2 mL) vanilla extract
7 egg whites
¹/₂ tsp cream of tartar (2 mL)
Vanilla Whey Frosting, page 64
(Double the recipe, if desired for a substantial frosting)

Yield: 16 servings
Single/Double Frosting
210.5/248.3 calories
10.1/13.5 g protein
15.5/17.8 g fat
7.3/8.3 g carbs

In large bowl, combine Vital Oat Ultimate Bake Mix, page 20, SPLENDA® Granular, baking powder, cinnamon, salt, nutmeg, allspice and cloves. Make a well in center. Pour in olive oil, egg yolks and Da Vinci® Sugar Free Vanilla Syrup. Beat with spoon until smooth.

In food processor with whipping assembly, beat egg whites with cream of tartar until very stiff. Pour cake batter very gradually over whipped egg whites and very gently fold in using rubber scraper (just until blended). Pour into greased tube cake pan (line with wax paper and spray with nonstick cooking spray, if pan is old, or if worried that cake may stick, as low-carb cakes often do). Bake in 325°F (160°C) oven 30 minutes. Increase heat to 350°F (180°C) and bake a further 10 minutes. Cool completely in pan on wire rack.

Vanilla Whey Frosting: Prepare as directed on page 64. Pour over cooled cake.

Helpful Hints: If you make a single batch of frosting and decide you want a double batch, it's no problem just to pour the new batch over the old one. A single amount of frosting will be able to be drizzled over the cake and not fully cover it in a thick layer.

CHEESECAKES

PEACHES AND CREAM CHEESECAKE

Deliciously creamy. Canned fruit cocktail may be used instead.

Graham Cracker-like Crust, page 41
$^2/_3$ cup Low-Carb Bake Mix, (150 mL)
  page 22
$^2/_3$ cup ground almonds (150 mL)
$^1/_3$ cup butter, melted (75 mL)
2 SPLENDA® packets
Filling:
32 oz regular cream cheese, (1 kg)
  softened
$^3/_4$ cup whipping cream (175 mL)
$1^2/_3$ cups SPLENDA® Granular (400 mL)
4 eggs
3 tbsp vital wheat gluten (45 mL)
2 tbsp vanilla extract (25 mL)
$1^1/_4$ cups canned peach slices, (300 mL)
  drained
Topping:
$1^1/_4$ cups Crème Fraiche, page 67 (300 mL)
$^1/_4$ cup canned peach slices, chopped (50 mL)

Yield: 16 servings
1 serving
369.0 calories
11.7 g protein
32.2 g fat
8.3 g carbs

Graham Cracker-like Crust: In medium bowl, combine Low-Carb Bake Mix, page 22, ground almonds, butter and SPLENDA®. Press into 9-inch (23 cm) glass pie dish. Bake in 350°F (180°C) oven 10 minutes, or until turning light brown.

Filling: In food processor with sharp blade or in bowl with electric mixer, process cream cheese. Add whipping cream and SPLENDA® Granular; process. While processing add eggs one at a time. Add vital wheat gluten and vanilla extract. Pour half cheesecake batter over prepared crust. Layer peaches on top. Pour remaining batter over peaches. Bake in 350°F (180°C) oven 40 to 45 minutes, or until turning light brown at edges. Let cool to room temperature. Chill. Before serving cover with Crème Fraiche, page 67 and garnish with chopped peaches, or peach slices.

Topping: Prepare Crème Fraiche, page 67.

LEMON CHEESECAKE

A tangy, citrus cheesecake. The crust is wonderfully substantial.

Short Crust:
1 cup Low-Carb Bake Mix, (250 mL)
  page 22
$^1/_4$ cup SPLENDA® Granular (50 mL)
6 tbsp butter, melted (90 mL)
Filling:
1 cup ricotta cheese (250 mL)
8 oz regular cream cheese, (250 g)
  softened
$1^1/_4$ cups SPLENDA® Granular (300 mL)
$^3/_4$ cup sour cream (175 mL)
2 egg yolks
$^1/_4$ cup lemon juice (50 mL)
1 tbsp finely grated lemon peel (15 mL)
2 drops yellow food coloring (optional)
2 egg whites
$^1/_8$ tsp cream of tartar (0.5 mL)
Topping:
$1^1/_4$ cups Crème Fraiche, page 67 (300 mL)
lemon slice for garnish

Yield: 12/16 servings
1 serving
275.8/206.9 calories
9.8/7.4 g protein
23.1/17.4 g fat
7.7/5.8 g carbs

Short Crust: In small bowl combine Low-Carb Bake Mix, page 22 and SPLENDA® Granular. Stir in butter. Press into 9-inch (23 cm) glass pie dish or springform pan. Bake in 350°F (180°C) oven 10 minutes.

Filling: In food processor with sharp blade or in blender, process ricotta cheese until smooth. Add cream cheese; process until smooth. Add SPLENDA® Granular, sour cream, egg yolks, lemon juice, lemon peel and yellow food coloring, if using; process until smooth. In bowl, beat egg whites and cream of tartar until stiff peaks form; fold into cheese mixture. Pour over cooled crust. Bake in 350°F (180°C) oven 40 to 45 minutes, or until set and browning slightly. Switch off oven and leave cheesecake inside until cool.

Topping: Spread Crème Fraiche over cooled cheesecake. Garnish center with twisted lemon slice. Refrigerate cheesecake.

Variations: Orange Cheesecake: Substitute orange juice and grated orange peel. (***7.9/5.9 g Carbs***)

Lime Cheesecake: Substitute lime juice and grated lime peel. (***7.7/5.8 g Carbs***)

STRAWBERRY CHEESECAKE

A delicious, fruity, lower-calorie cheesecake.

Almond Crust:
1 cup ground almonds (250 mL)
1 SPLENDA® packet
1 egg white
Filling:
2 cups ricotta cheese (500 mL)
8 oz light cream cheese, softened (250 g)
1¼ cups SPLENDA® Granular (300 mL)
1 cup plain yogurt (250 mL)
2 tbsp vital wheat gluten (25 mL)
1 tsp vanilla extract (5 mL)
¼ tsp salt (1 mL)
3 eggs
Strawberry Sauce:
2 cups frozen unsweetened strawberries (500 mL)
¼ cup SPLENDA® Granular (50 mL)
3 tbsp water (45 mL)
½ tsp Thickening Agent, page 66 (2 mL)

Yield: 12/16 servings
1 serving
200.9/150.7 calories
9.1/6.8 g protein
14.2/10.6 g fat
8.4/6.3 g carbs

Almond Crust: In small bowl, combine ground almonds, SPLENDA® and egg white. Spread in 9-inch (23 cm) springform pan or glass pie dish. Cover with plastic wrap. Press crust out evenly; remove wrap. Bake in 350°F (180°C) oven 10 minutes. Cover with foil and bake another 5 minutes.

Filling: In food processor with sharp blade or in blender, process ricotta cheese until smooth. Add cream cheese; process. Add SPLENDA® Granular, yogurt, vital wheat gluten, vanilla extract and salt. While processing, add eggs one at a time and process just until well combined. Pour over crust and bake in 350°F (180°C) oven 45 to 50 minutes, or until center is softly set. Set aside to cool.

Strawberry Sauce: In medium saucepan, combine strawberries, SPLENDA® Granular, water and Thickening agent, page 66. Bring to boil. Set aside to cool. Pour over cooled cheesecake.

Variation: Raspberry Cheesecake: Use frozen unsweetened raspberries. (*8.0/6.0 g Carbs*)

ALMOND CHOCOLATE CHEESECAKE
A popular flavor combination in a firm cheesecake.

Almond Crust:
1 cup ground almonds (250 mL)
1 SPLENDA® packet
1 egg white
Filling:
24 oz light cream cheese (750 g)
1 1/2 cups SPLENDA® Granular (375 mL)
1 cup sour cream (250 mL)
1/3 cup Dutch cocoa (75 mL)
1/4 cup almond butter (50 mL)
2 eggs
1/4 cup Da Vinci® Sugar Free Chocolate Syrup (50 mL)
1 tbsp vital wheat gluten, OR oat flour (15 mL)
Topping:
1 cup Crème Fraiche, page 67 (250 mL)

Yield: 12/16 servings
1 serving
328.6/246.5 calories
10.5/7.9 g protein
28.3/21.2 g fat
8.9/6.7 g carbs

Almond Crust: In small bowl, combine ground almonds, SPLENDA® and egg white. Spread in 9-inch (23 cm) springform pan. Cover with plastic wrap. Press crust out evenly; remove wrap. Bake in 350°F (180°C) oven 10 minutes. Cover with foil and bake another 5 minutes.

Filling: In food processor with sharp blade, blender or in bowl with electric mixer, process cream cheese until smooth. Add SPLENDA® Granular, sour cream, Dutch cocoa, almond butter and eggs. Process until smooth. Add Da Vinci® Sugar Free Chocolate Syrup; process. Add vital wheat gluten; process. Bake in 350°F (180°C) oven 45 minutes, or until set at edges and just softly set in center. Chill cheesecake and then spread topping over it.

Topping: Prepare Crème Fraiche as directed on page 67.

Variations: Peanut Butter Chocolate Cheesecake: Substitute sugarless, salt free peanut butter. (***8.8/6.6 g Carbs***)

Da Vinci® Alternative: Use whipping cream instead and a couple of SPLENDA® packets and 1 tsp (5 mL) chocolate extract. (***9.3/7.0 g Carbs***)

Helpful Hints: Idea for garnishing cheesecake: Place narrow strips of waxed paper at an angle over top of cheesecake leaving spaces between them. Sift a mixture of cocoa and SPLENDA® Granular (small amount mixed together) over top. Remove paper and chill.

CHOCOLATE CHIP CHEESECAKE
Fabulous milk chocolate cheesecake studded with chocolate chips.

Almond Crust:
1 cup ground almonds (250 mL)
1 SPLENDA® packet
1 egg white
Filling:
1 cup ricotta cheese (250 mL)
16 oz regular cream cheese, (500 g)
  softened
1¹/₂ cups SPLENDA® Granular (375 mL)
¹/₃ cup Dutch cocoa (75 mL)
¹/₄ cup sour cream (50 mL)
2 tsp vanilla extract (10 mL)
¹/₈ tsp salt (0.5 mL)
3 eggs
1 cup sugarless chocolate chips, (250 mL)
  (sweetened)

Yield: 12/16 servings
1 serving
320.6/240.5 calories
10.5 g/7.8 g protein
24.6 g/18.5 g fat
7.3 g/5.5 g carbs

Almond Crust: In small bowl, combine ground almonds, SPLENDA® and egg white. Spread in bottom of 9-inch (23 cm) springform pan. Cover with plastic wrap and press out evenly; remove wrap. Bake in 350°F (180°C) oven 10 minutes. Cover with foil and bake 5 more minutes.

Filling: In food processor with sharp blade or in blender, process ricotta cheese until smooth. Add cream cheese; process. Add SPLENDA® Granular, Dutch cocoa, sour cream, vanilla extract and salt. Add eggs one at a time while processing, just until combined. Stir in chocolate chips. Spray sides of springform pan with nonstick cooking spray. Pour cheesecake batter over baked crust.

Bake in 350°F (180°C) oven 40 to 45 minutes, or until firmly set around edges and softly set in center.

Variation: Chocolate Raisin Cheesecake: Omit chocolate chips and substitute ¹/₂ cup (125 mL) plump, seedless California raisins, snipped in half.
Yield: 16 servings. 1 serving: *(8.7 g Carbs)*

~~Low-Carb Dieting Tip~~
Sugar ages one. It slowly damages tissues such as collagen inside the body.

NEW YORK CHEESECAKE
A classic and a favorite!

Short Crust:
1 cup Low-Carb Bake Mix, (250 mL)
  page 22
$^1/_4$ cup SPLENDA® Granular (50 mL)
6 tbsp butter, melted (90 mL)
Filling:
16 oz regular cream cheese, (500 g)
  softened
8 oz light cream cheese, (250 g)
  softened
$1^1/_4$ cups SPLENDA® Granular (300 mL)
1 tbsp lemon juice (15 mL)
3 tbsp vital wheat gluten (45 mL)
2 tsp finely grated orange peel (10 mL)
2 tsp finely grated lemon peel (10 mL)
4 eggs
$^1/_2$ cup whipping cream (125 mL)
Garnish: (optional)
Crème Fraiche, page 67
Canned mandarin orange segments

Yield: 12/16 servings
1 serving
339.6/254.7 calories
12.7 g/9.5 g protein
29.4 g/22.0 g fat
6.7/5.0 g carbs

Short Crust: In small bowl combine Low-Carb Bake Mix, page 22 and SPLENDA® Granular. Stir in butter. Press into 9-inch (23 cm) springform pan. Bake in 350°F (180°C) oven 10 minutes.

Filling: In food processor with sharp blade, blender or in bowl with electric mixer, process cream cheeses until smooth. Add SPLENDA® Granular, lemon juice, vital wheat gluten, orange peel and lemon peel. While processing add eggs, one at a time, processing just until combined. Add cream; process. Spray insides of springform pan with nonstick cooking spray. Pour cheesecake batter over prepared crust. Bake in 300°F (150°C) oven 1 hour. Run knife around circumference. Leave in oven until cool. Refrigerate.

Garnish (optional): Just before serving place large dollops of Crème Fraiche, page 67 around perimeter of cheesecake. Place one mandarin orange segment on each dollop, if desired. Otherwise, simply sprinkle top of cheesecake with toasted, sliced almonds, grated unsweetened chocolate, chocolate drizzle, page 168, *Splendid Low-Carbing*, or any other creative topping. This cheesecake is really phenomenal with Strawberry Sauce, page 55 as a topping.

VANILLA CHEESECAKE

A superb, plain cheesecake with a firm texture.

Graham Cracker-like Crust:
²/₃ cup Low-Carb Bake Mix, (150 mL)
  page 22
²/₃ cup ground almonds (150 mL)
¹/₃ cup butter, melted (75 mL)
2 SPLENDA® packets

Filling:
1 cup ricotta cheese (250 mL)
16 oz regular cream cheese (500 g)
1¹/₄ cups SPLENDA® Granular (300 mL)
¹/₄ cup whipping cream (50 mL)
3 tbsp vital wheat gluten (45 mL)
1 tbsp vanilla extract (15 mL)
¹/₈ tsp salt (0.5 mL)
4 eggs

Topping:
1 cup sour cream (250 mL)
2 SPLENDA® packets
2 tsp lemon juice (10 mL)
¹/₂ tsp vanilla extract (2 mL)

Yield: 12/16 servings
1 serving
352.7/264.5 calories
13.3/10.0 g protein
29.9/22.4 g fat
7.7 g/5.7 g carbs

Graham Cracker-like Crust: In medium bowl, combine Low-Carb Bake Mix, page 22, ground almonds, butter and SPLENDA®. Press into 9-inch (23 cm) glass pie dish. Bake in 350°F (180°C) oven 10 minutes, or until turning brown.

Filling: In food processor with sharp blade or in blender, process ricotta cheese until smooth. Add cream cheese; process. Add SPLENDA® Granular, whipping cream, vital wheat gluten, vanilla extract and salt. While processing add eggs one at a time, until combined. Pour over prepared crust. Bake in 300°F (150°C) oven 1 hour. Spread sour cream topping over cheesecake. Bake another 10 minutes.

Topping: In small bowl, combine sour cream, SPLENDA®, lemon juice and vanilla extract.

Helpful Hints: For a sweeter cheesecake, add an extra ¹/₄ cup (50 mL) SPLENDA® Granular, or replace whipping cream with Da Vinci® Sugar Free Vanilla Syrup. **Extra garnishing ideas for a special occasion:** If desired, garnish further with Chocolate Drizzle, page 168, *Splendid Low-Carbing* and sprinkle with grated unsweetened chocolate. Garnish sides with Crème Fraiche, page 67. Use enough Thickening Agent, page 66 to form a stiff Crème Fraiche.

CHOCOLATE ORANGE MARBLE CHEESECAKE

I served this after Christmas dinner. Everyone thought it was excellent.

Short Crust:
1 cup Low-Carb Bake Mix, (250 mL)
  page 22
$^1/_4$ cup SPLENDA® Granular (50 mL)
6 tbsp butter, melted (90 mL)
Filling:
24 oz regular cream cheese (750 g)
$1^1/_4$ cups SPLENDA® Granular (300 mL)
3 eggs
4 oz sugarless chocolate chips, (120 g)
  (sweetened), melted
2 SPLENDA® packets
2 tbsp Da Vinci® Sugar Free (25 mL)
  Orange Syrup
2 tbsp vital wheat gluten (25 mL)
1 tbsp finely grated orange peel (15 mL)

Yield: 12/16 servings
1 serving
366.5/274.9 calories
12.3/9.2 g protein
30.1/22.5 g fat
6.9/5.2 g carbs

Short Crust: In small bowl combine Low-Carb Bake Mix, page 22 and SPLENDA® Granular. Stir in butter. Press into 9-inch (23 cm) springform pan. Bake in 350°F (180°C) oven 10 minutes.

Filling: In food processor with sharp blade, blender or in bowl with electric mixer, process cream cheese. Add SPLENDA® Granular and while processing add eggs one at a time, until smooth. Remove 1 cup of cheesecake batter; stir in chocolate and SPLENDA®. Set aside. To remaining cheesecake batter, add Da Vinci® Sugar Free Orange Syrup, vital wheat gluten and orange peel; process. Pour orange batter over crust. Top with spoonfuls of chocolate batter. Drag small knife through batters for a marbled effect.

Bake in 300°F (150°C) oven 50 minutes. Run knife around edge. Switch off oven and leave cheesecake inside until completely cool. Remove springform ring, cover cheesecake with plastic wrap and refrigerate. If desired, just before serving, place cheesecake on dinner plate on cake stand and garnish sides with Crème Fraiche, page 67. Sprinkle lightly with grated unsweetened chocolate.

Variation: Da Vinci® Alternative: Omit the syrup and also vital wheat gluten. Add 2 tsp (10 mL) orange extract. (***6.7/5.1 g Carbs***). Alternatively, substitute 2 tbsp (25 mL) orange juice from concentrate, if desired, and keep the vital wheat gluten. (***8.0/5.9 g Carbs***)

Helpful Hint: Chocolate Mixture, page 62 may be used instead.

BLUEBERRY SWIRL CHEESECAKE

Everyone agreed that this cheesecake is superbly delicious and very beautiful.

Short Crust:
1 cup Low-Carb Bake Mix, (250 mL)
  page 22
$^1/_4$ cup SPLENDA® Granular (50 mL)
6 tbsp butter, melted (90 mL)
Filling:
32 oz regular cream cheese (1 kg)
40 SPLENDA® packets, OR
  $1^2/_3$ cups SPLENDA® Granular (400 mL)
$^1/_2$ cup sour cream (125 mL)
4 eggs
2 tbsp vanilla extract (25 mL)
Blueberry Puree:
$1^3/_4$ cups frozen unsweetened blueberries (425 mL)
3 tbsp water (45 mL)
2 tsp lemon juice (10 mL)
$^3/_4$ tsp Thickening Agent, page 66 (3 mL)
4 SPLENDA® packets

Yield: 16 servings
1 serving
311.3 calories
10.3 g protein
26.4 g fat
7.8 g carbs

Short Crust: In small bowl combine Low-Carb Bake Mix, page 22 and SPLENDA® Granular. Stir in butter. Press into 9-inch (23 cm) springform pan. Bake in 350°F (180°C) oven 10 minutes.

Filling: In food processor with sharp blade or in bowl with electric mixer, process cream cheese. Add SPLENDA® and sour cream; process. While processing, add eggs one at a time, as well as vanilla extract. Scrape sides occasionally. Spray sides of springform pan with nonstick cooking spray. Pour cheesecake batter over prepared crust. Drop 6 large dollops of Blueberry Puree over top. Using a dinner knife, drag it through Blueberry Puree and cheesecake batter, to create a beautiful, marbled effect on top. Bake in 300°F (150°C) oven 50 minutes to 1 hour, or until just beginning to show signs of turning brown at edges. Run thin knife between cheesecake and pan. When cooled, refrigerate.

Blueberry Puree: In microwaveable container, cook blueberries, water, lemon juice and Thickening Agent, page 66, 3 minutes, stirring halfway through. Pour into blender along with SPLENDA®. Blend until smooth.

~~Low-Carb Dieting Tip~~
Exercise is wonderful for your mental attitude.

CAPPUCCINO CHOCOLATE SWIRL CHEESECAKE

This fabulous cheesecake has a popular flavor combination.

Short Crust:
1 cup Low-Carb Bake Mix, (250 mL)
  page 22
$^1/_4$ cup SPLENDA® Granular (50 mL)
6 tbsp butter, melted (90 mL)
Filling:
32 oz regular cream cheese, (1 kg)
  softened
40 SPLENDA® packets, OR
  $1^2/_3$ cups SPLENDA® Granular (400 mL)
$^1/_2$ cup sour cream (125 mL)
4 eggs at room temperature
1 tbsp instant coffee granules (15 ml)
1 tbsp hot water (15 mL)
1 tsp vanilla extract (5 mL)
Chocolate Mixture:*
3 tbsp Dutch cocoa (45 mL)
4 SPLENDA® packets
1 tbsp whipping cream (15 mL)
1 tbsp Da Vinci® Sugar Free Chocolate Syrup, OR whipping cream (15 mL)

Yield: 12/16 servings
1 serving
408.3/306.3 calories
13.9 g/10.5 g protein
35.6 g/26.7 g fat
8.5 g/6.4 g carbs

Short Crust: In small bowl combine Low-Carb Bake Mix, page 22 and SPLENDA® Granular. Stir in butter. Press into 9-inch (23 cm) springform pan. Bake in 350°F (180°C) oven 10 minutes.

Filling: In food processor with sharp blade or with electric mixer, process cream cheese. Add SPLENDA® and sour cream; process. While processing, add eggs one at a time. Remove 1 cup (250 mL) batter. Stir in chocolate mixture. To remaining batter add coffee (mixed with hot water to dissolve) and vanilla extract; process. Drop 6 large spoonfuls of chocolate mixture on top of batter. Drag small knife through chocolate to swirl. Bake in 350°F (180°C) oven 45 minutes, or until top is light brown and center is slightly soft. Cool on rack, then chill. Garnish with Crème Fraiche, page 67, if desired around outside of cake.

Chocolate Mixture: In small bowl, combine cocoa, SPLENDA®, 1 tbsp (15 mL) whipping cream and Da Vinci® Sugar Free Chocolate Syrup or 1 tbsp (15 mL) whipping cream.

Helpful Hint: *If desired, use 3 oz (90 g) sugarless chocolate chips, melted, instead of the chocolate mixture. This will be sweeter (*8.4/6.3 g Carbs*)

RASPBERRY LEMON CHEESECAKE
A smooth, creamy, solid cheesecake high on flavor.

Graham Cracker-like Crust:
$^2/_3$ cup Low-Carb Bake Mix, (150 mL)
  page 22
$^2/_3$ cup ground almonds (150 mL)
$^1/_3$ cup butter, melted (75 mL)
2 SPLENDA® packets

Filling:
32 oz regular cream cheese, (1 kg)
  softened
$1^1/_2$ cups SPLENDA® Granular (375 mL)
$^3/_4$ cup sour cream (175 mL)
3 tbsp vital wheat gluten (45 mL)
2 tbsp lemon juice (25 mL)
2 tbsp Da Vinci® French Vanilla Syrup (25 mL)
1 tbsp finely grated lemon peel (15 ml)
4 eggs

Raspberry Topping:
3 cups frozen unsweetened raspberries (750 mL)
6 SPLENDA® packets
2 tsp lemon juice (10 mL)
$^1/_2$ tsp Thickening Agent, page 66 (2 mL)

Yield: 16 servings
1 serving
316.5 calories
11.3 g protein
26.6 g fat
7.6 g carbs

Graham Cracker-like Crust: In medium bowl, combine Low-Carb Bake Mix, page 22, ground almonds, butter and SPLENDA®. Press into 9-inch (23 cm) glass pie dish. Bake in 350°F (180°C) oven 10 minutes, or until turning brown.

Filling: In food processor with sharp blade or in bowl with electric mixer, process cream cheese. Add SPLENDA® Granular and sour cream; process. Add vital wheat gluten, lemon juice, Da Vinci® French Vanilla Syrup and lemon peel. While processing, add eggs one at a time until incorporated. Pour over crust. Bake in 350°F (180°C) oven 45 minutes, or until just beginning to turn brown at edges. Carefully pour Raspberry Topping over top of cooled cheesecake. Chill.

Raspberry Topping: In large saucepan, combine raspberries, SPLENDA®, lemon juice and Thickening Agent, page 66. Bring to boil. Let cool slightly.

Variations: Bumble Berry Lemon Cheesecake: Use a frozen unsweetened mixture of blackberries, raspberries and blueberries. (***8.4 g Carbs***)

Da Vinci® Alternative: Use 1 tbsp (15 mL) vanilla extract and 1 tbsp (15 mL) water or an extra tablespoon (15 mL) lemon juice and extra sweetener to taste.

CONFECTIONS & FROSTINGS

VANILLA WHEY FROSTING

Condensed milk-like and toffee-like. This is an improved version of the frosting in Splendid Low-Carbing for Life, Vol. 1.

$3/4$ cup vanilla whey protein (175 mL)
3 tbsp skim milk powder, OR (45 mL)
  whole milk powder
6 SPLENDA® packets
$1/4$ cup Da Vinci® Sugar Free (50 mL)
  French Vanilla or Vanilla Syrup
3 tbsp butter, melted (45 mL)

Yield: 12/16 servings
1 serving
56.1/42.4 calories
4.6 g/3.4 g protein
3.6 g/2.7 g fat
1.5 g/1.1 g carbs

In medium bowl, combine vanilla whey protein, whole or skim milk powder and SPLENDA®. With metal spoon, stir in Da Vinci® Sugar Free French Vanilla or Vanilla Syrup and butter. Blend smooth in blender. This frosting gets poured on, rather than spread on the cake, however, some spreading is possible with a flat knife, before it sets. Work quickly.

Variations: **Create-a-Flavor Whey Frosting:** Use any flavor whey protein with Da Vinci® Sugar Free Syrup of choice. For example, use vanilla whey protein with Da Vinci® Sugar Free White Chocolate Syrup for a White Chocolate Whey Frosting.

Chocolate Vanilla Whey Frosting: Use vanilla whey protein, Da Vinci® Sugar Free Chocolate Syrup, 1 tbsp (15 mL) whole milk powder and 2 tbsp (25 mL) Dutch cocoa. (***1.1 g/0.8 g Carbs***)

Da Vinci® Alternative: Use $3^1/2$ tbsp (52 mL) water, 1 tsp (5 mL) vanilla extract and an extra SPLENDA® packet, or to taste.

Helpful Hint: For a Bundt Cake, double the frosting for a truly decadent topping.

~~Low-Carb Dieting Tip~~
Trans fats and not saturated fats are linked to elevated cholesterol and heart disease. Saturated fats are not bad, as we've been led to believe.

STICKY CHOCOLATE TOFFEE

High protein, sticky toffee is one of my favorite sweet treats. 5 Pieces will give you more protein than 2 eggs. It is also so quick and easy to make.

Vanilla Whey Frosting, page 64
  (double the recipe and use 24
  SPLENDA® packets. No need to use
  blender)
2 oz unsweetened chocolate (60 g)

Yield: 36 squares
1 square
43.1 calories
3.1 g protein
2.9 g fat
1.5 g carbs

In medium bowl, prepare Vanilla Whey Frosting, page 64. In cereal bowl, microwave chocolate 2 minutes; stir until completely melted. Stir into frosting or add to frosting in blender and blend until smooth. Turn out into 8-inch (20 cm) square glass baking dish. Cover dish with plastic wrap (do not place plastic in contact with toffee). Freeze. Microwave 15 to 20 seconds to enjoy.

Variations: **Sticky Vanilla Caramel Toffee:** Use 2 oz (60 g) cocoa butter, melted, instead of unsweetened baking chocolate. Very sticky business – work quickly! (*1.2 g Carbs*)

Sticky Coconut Milk Chocolate Toffee: Use 1 oz (30 g) cocoa butter and 1 oz (30 g) unsweetened baking chocolate, melted and substitute Da Vinci® Sugar Free Coconut Syrup in the frosting. (*1.4 g Carbs*)

CONFECTIONER'S SUGAR SUBSTITUTE

This is an easier recipe than the one in my previous books.

2¼ cups SPLENDA® Granular (550 mL)
1⅓ cups whole milk powder* (325 mL)
⅔ cup vanilla whey protein (150 mL)

Yield: 4 cups (1 L)
1 tbsp (15 mL) per serving
19.7 calories
1.4 g protein
0.7 g fat
1.9 g carbs

In large bowl, combine SPLENDA® Granular, whole milk powder and vanilla whey protein.

Helpful Hint: *Skim milk powder may be used instead, however, blend finely in small batches in blender first, before combining with remaining ingredients.

THICKENING AGENT

This is useful to use instead of pure cornstarch or flour in thickening sauces.

$8^{1}/_{2}$ tsp xanthan gum (42 mL)
$4^{1}/_{2}$ tsp guar gum (22 mL)
$2^{1}/_{4}$ tsp corn starch (11 mL)

> **Yield:** $^{1}/_{3}$ cup (75 mL)
> 1 tsp (5 mL) per serving
> 1.5 calories
> 0.0 g protein
> 0.0 g fat
> **0.4 g carbs**

In small plastic container with lid, combine xanthan gum, guar gum and cornstarch; seal. Shake well. Store at room temperature.

Helpful Hints: Substitute Thickening Agent for cornstarch, using $^{1}/_{4}$ as much and substitute Thickening Agent for flour, using $^{1}/_{8}$ as much to achieve approximately the same results.

This Thickening Agent must be used in small quantities to avoid a "gummy" texture.

You may use only guar gum or only xanthan gum, if one or the other is not available.

Thickening Agent is utilized frequently throughout this cookbook; however, if you would like the convenience of a commercial product, then use "ThickenThin not/Starch" by Expert Foods (http://expertfoods.com). Things come out more or less the same. It is widely available at upscale health food stores and online.

~~Low-Carb Dieting Health Alert~~

Folic acid supplementation for women of childbearing age prevents birth defects such as spina bifida and prevents a common childhood cancer, neuroblastoma. Since low-carbers are no longer consuming white flour and pasta (purposefully enriched with folic acid) or orange juice, this supplementation is essential. During the period immediately following conception, the fetus is extremely vulnerable to a shortage of folic acid in the mother.

CRÈME FRAICHE

Lovely sweetened whipped topping for serving with desserts or for garnishing desserts. It holds up better than plain whipped cream and tastes better. Double Thickening agent, page 66, for thicker Crème Fraiche.

1 cup whipping cream (250 mL)
$\frac{1}{2}$ cup SPLENDA® Granular (125 mL)
$\frac{1}{4}$ tsp Thickening Agent, page 66 (1 mL)
  (optional)
$\frac{2}{3}$ cup regular sour cream, OR (150 mL)
  nonfat sour cream
$\frac{1}{2}$ tsp vanilla extract (2 mL)

> **Yield:** $2\frac{1}{8}$ cups (525 mL)
> 2 tbsp (25 mL) per serving
> 56.2 calories
> 0.5 g protein
> 5.4 g fat
> **1.5 g carbs**

In food processor, on low speed, process whipping cream with SPLENDA® Granular. While processing, sprinkle in Thickening Agent, page 66, if using, through feed tube. Process until thick. Add sour cream and vanilla extract; process on medium high speed just until combined. It will keep at least one week or longer in the refrigerator.

Variation: **Lower Carb Alternative:** Omit SPLENDA® Granular. Use $\frac{1}{2}$ tsp (2 mL) to $\frac{3}{4}$ tsp (3 mL) Thickening Agent, page 66. Use $\frac{1}{4}$ cup (50 mL) Da Vinci® Sugar Free Syrup such as Vanilla or French Vanilla instead of SPLENDA® Granular. Process whipping cream and Thickening Agent until thick. Add syrup along with sour cream; process on medium high speed. Add extra $\frac{1}{4}$ tsp (1 mL) Thickening Agent, page 66, if necessary, as well.
2 tbsp (25 mL) per serving: (53.6 calories, 0.5 g protein, 5.4 g fat, ***0.8 g carbs***)

Helpful Hints: Thickening Agent, page 66, makes Crème Fraiche firmer and easier to garnish desserts using a pastry bag.

This topping is wonderful on fresh fruit salad or fresh strawberries and on a myriad of desserts. In my opinion, it tastes better than sweetened whipped cream. Recipe may easily be doubled or halved.

Half this recipe will suffice as a topping for a cheesecake.
Yield: 12 servings. 1 serving: (42.0 calories, 0.4 g protein, 4.1 g fat, ***1.1 g carbs***)

~~Low-Carb Dieting Tip~~
Losing weight is one thing and it is another thing learning how to maintain one's weight loss effectively.

CONDENSED MILK

Be prepared for a delicious surprise – very similar in consistency and taste to the real thing! This recipe will be useful in some of your old favorite desserts.

$^1/_3$ cup whipping cream (75 mL)
$^1/_3$ cup butter, melted (75 mL)
3 tbsp water (45 mL)
$^1/_2$ tsp vanilla extract (2 mL)
$^2/_3$ cup SPLENDA® Granular (150 mL)
$^1/_3$ cup vanilla whey protein (75 mL)
$^1/_3$ cup whole milk powder, OR (75 mL)
  skim milk powder
$^1/_8$ tsp Thickening Agent, (0.5 mL)
  page 66

Yield: 1$^1/_8$ cups (275 mL)
1 tbsp (15 mL) per serving
65.8 calories
2.0 g protein
5.6 g fat
2.0 g carbs

In blender, place whipping cream, butter, water, vanilla extract, SPLENDA® Granular, vanilla whey protein, whole milk powder and Thickening Agent, page 66. Blend until smooth. (My previous cookbooks used softened butter, but melted is better, producing a smoother result.)

Variation: **Lower Carb Alternative:** Use 2 tbsp (25 mL) whipping cream, 1 tbsp (15 mL) water and $^1/_3$ cup (75 mL) Da Vinci® Sugar Free Caramel, French Vanilla or Dulce De Leche Syrup. Omit SPLENDA® Granular, however, add 1 SPLENDA® packet, if desired. Increase Thickening Agent to $^1/_4$ tsp (1 mL). 1 tbsp (15mL): (53.4 calories, 2.0 g protein, 4.79 g fat (77.8%), *1.0 g carbs*)

CHOCOLATE STRAWBERRY SPREAD

There are many uses for this delicious spread.

$^2/_3$ cup chocolate chips, (150 mL)
  sugar free (sweetened)
$^1/_3$ cup strawberry fruit (75 mL)
  spread, sugar free, OR raspberry
  fruit spread (sieved to remove seeds)

Yield: $^2/_3$ cup (150 mL)
1 tsp (5 mL) per serving
18.9 calories
0.2 g protein
0.9 g fat
0.6 g carbs

In double boiler, melt chocolate chips. Stir in strawberry fruit spread.

Helpful Hint: This spread is great spread over brownies, cookies, as a filling for double-layered cakes, for spreading on pancakes, etc.

CARAMEL SAUCE

Such an easy sauce, with a super taste and smooth, thick texture. Make this sauce the day before, or see helpful hints below or the instant variation. Also see page 71 – just use Da Vinci® Sugar Free Caramel Syrup and cocoa butter.

$^1/_3$ cup whipping cream (75 mL)
$^1/_3$ cup butter, melted (75 mL)
$^2/_3$ cup SPLENDA® Granular (150 mL)
$^1/_3$ cup boiling water (75 mL)
1 Vanilla Caramel tea bag
  (Bigelow®)
$^1/_3$ cup vanilla whey protein (75 mL)
$^1/_3$ cup whole milk powder, OR (75 mL)
  skim milk powder
$^1/_2$ oz cocoa butter, melted (15 g)
  (melt 2 minutes in microwave oven)

Yield: 1$^1/_3$ cups (325 mL) 1 tbsp (15 mL) per serving 54.7 calories 1.6 g protein 4.7 g fat ***1.7 g carbs***

In blender, combine whipping cream, melted butter and SPLENDA® Granular. Pour boiling water into teacup. Add tea bag. Steep 5 minutes. Remove tea bag. Pour tea into blender. Add vanilla whey protein, whole milk powder and cocoa butter. Blend. Pour into a container and refrigerate until very well chilled and thickened.

Variation: **Instant Caramel Sauce:** Use 2 tbsp (25 mL) of the steeped tea and 3 tbsp (45 mL) Da Vinci® Sugar Free Caramel Syrup. This sauce will be thick enough (due to thickeners in syrup) without chilling. When chilled, on the other hand, it will become too thick and will need to be blended again with a little water or cream to the right consistency.

Helpful Hints: If you are going to use the main recipe Caramel Sauce right away, then use only $^1/_4$ cup (50 mL) water and $^1/_8$ tsp (0.5 mL) Thickening Agent, page 66. Double Thickening Agent, if sauce is still not thick enough for your taste. If by chance (and this shouldn't really happen) you get a bit of a "tea" taste from the tannin in the tea in the main recipe, reduce the steeping time by 2 minutes the next time around, or use less tea and some water.

Heating this sauce is not recommended. For more of a hardening effect of the sauce when poured on ice cream, use 1 oz (30 g) cocoa butter, melted.

~~Low-Carb Dieting Tip~~
Addictions can be managed only through abstaining from the offending food.

CHOCOLATE SAUCE AND FROSTING

This sauce is delicious. See page 71 for another delicious chocolate sauce that does not rely on chocolate chips.

1 cup sugarless chocolate chips (250 mL) (sweetened)
1 can Thick Cream, (170 mL) Carnation® (25% M.F.)
1 tbsp Da Vinci® Sugar Free (15 mL) Kahuli Caffe or B-52 Syrup (optional)

Yield: 1 cup (250 mL)
1 tbsp (15 mL) per serving
74.2 calories
0.7 g protein
5.3 g fat
0.9 g carbs

In medium microwaveable bowl with lid, nuke chocolate and cream 2 minutes. Stir to combine well. Stir in Da Vinci® Sugar Free Kahuli Caffe or B-52 Syrup, if using. If using as a frosting, refrigerate or briefly freeze sauce, until it has a firmer consistency and spreads easily.

Helpful Hints: Use warm chocolate sauce for dipping fruits or as a topping for ice cream. This would make an awesome topping for a cheesecake or pour over a crust and then add a pie or cheesecake filling.

Use this thick sauce as a delicious, decadent drizzle over plain cakes or any other dessert that it would compliment.

Use this sauce as a frosting for brownies or cakes. It is also great for frosting cookies. Use this sauce as the basis of chocolate truffles as this sauce is similar to ganache (a smooth mixture of chocolate and cream).

Variation: **French Silk Pie:** For a really decadent, famous pie, double recipe and pour over a Short Crust, page 54 or Graham Cracker-like Crust, page 41, and let set 24 hours in refrigerator. For a firmer pie, drain cream first over a colander and add extra cream from another can to make up for lost volume. ***Yield:*** 10/12 servings. (350.2/291.9 calories, 6.5/5.4 g protein, 24.0/22.5 g fat, 4.4/3.7 g carbs)

Helpful Hint: The frosting is a little sparse for a double-layered cake, however, with a filling for the middle of the cake, such as custard or cream whipped with cocoa and sweetener, it is then substantial and able to frost the entire cake comfortably.

~~Low-Carb Dieting Tip~~
Find substitutes for old favorites that you feel you cannot do without.

CONDENSED MILK CHOCOLATE SAUCE

Use any Da Vinci® Sugar Free Syrup to create your own sauces and frostings.

$^1/_2$ cup whipping cream (125 mL)
$^1/_3$ cup butter, melted (75 mL)
$^1/_3$ cup Da Vinci® Sugar Free (75 mL)
  French Vanilla or Vanilla Syrup
1 cup SPLENDA® Granular (250 mL)
$^1/_3$ cup vanilla whey protein (75 mL)
$^1/_3$ cup skim milk powder, OR (75 mL)
  whole milk powder
$^1/_8$ tsp Thickening Agent, page 66 (0.5 mL)
1 oz unsweetened chocolate, melted (30 g)

> **Yield:** $1^2/_3$ cups (400 mL)
> 1 tbsp (15 mL) per serving
> 51.1 calories
> 1.4 g protein
> 4.5 g fat
> *1.7 g carbs*

In blender, combine whipping cream, butter, Da Vinci® Sugar Free French Vanilla or Vanilla Syrup, SPLENDA® Granular, vanilla whey protein, skim or whole milk powder and Thickening Agent, page 66. Blend until smooth. Add melted chocolate; blend. Serve immediately or refrigerate and use later.

Variations: **Condensed Milk Chocolate Frosting:** Use $^1/_3$ cup (75 mL) whipping cream and 2 tbsp (25 mL) Da Vinci® Sugar Free Vanilla Syrup. Yield: 1 cup (250 mL). 12/16 servings:
100.5/75.4 calories, 2.9/2.2 g protein, 8.6/6.4 g fat, 3.7/2.8 g carbs.

White Chocolate Sauce/Frosting: Substitute Da Vinci® Sugar Free White Chocolate Syrup in main recipe and use cocoa butter instead of chocolate. Follow instructions for variation above for frosting.

MOLASSES SUBSTITUTE

Use this recipe anywhere regular molasses is required.

1 cup SPLENDA® Granular (250 mL)
$1^1/_2$ cups water (375 mL)
2 tbsp butter (25 mL)
2 tbsp molasses (25 mL)
1 tsp Thickening Agent, page 66 (5 mL)
$^1/_8$ tsp salt (0.5 mL)

> **Yield:** $1^1/_2$ cups (375 mL)
> 1 tbsp (15 mL) per serving
> 16.9 calories
> 0.0 g protein
> 1.0 g fat
> *2.1 g carbs*

In medium saucepan, combine SPLENDA® Granular, water, butter, molasses, Thickening Agent, page 66 and salt. Bring to boil. Sieve.

ORANGE CHEESE FROSTING

Great for loaves or doubled for a layer cake or to frost cookies.

$^1/_4$ cup cottage cheese, OR (50 mL)
  ricotta cheese
$2^1/_2$ oz cream cheese (75 g)
$^1/_4$ cup SPLENDA® Granular (50 mL)
1 tbsp orange juice concentrate (15 mL)
1 tbsp unsalted butter (15 mL)
1 tsp finely grated orange peel (5 mL)

> *Yield:* 18 servings
> 1 serving
> 36.2 calories
> 1.2 g protein
> 2.9 g fat
> *1.4 g carbs*

In food processor with sharp blade, or in blender, process cottage cheese or ricotta cheese until smooth. Add cream cheese, SPLENDA® Granular, orange juice concentrate, butter and orange peel; process until smooth.

Variations: **Orange Cheese Frosting for double-layer cake:** Double above recipe. 12 servings: (*2.8 g Carbs*)

Lemon Cheese Frosting: Use 1 tbsp (15 mL) lemon juice and 1 tsp (5 mL) finely grated lemon peel. 18 servings: (*1.0 g Carbs*)

Lemon Cheese Frosting for double-layer cake: Double the Lemon Cheese Frosting. 12 servings: (*1.8 g Carbs*)

VANILLA COCONUT TOFFEE

A chewy confection that is solid at refrigerator temperature.

3 oz cream cheese, softened (90 g)
2 tbsp whipping cream (25 mL)
2 tbsp whole milk powder, OR (25 mL)
  skim milk powder
2 tsp vanilla extract (10 mL)
1 cup vanilla whey protein (250 mL)
1 cup desiccated coconut (250 mL)
$^2/_3$ cup SPLENDA® Granular (150 mL)
1 oz cocoa butter, melted (30 g)

> *Yield:* 36 servings
> 1 serving
> 47.7 calories
> 2.3 g protein
> 3.6 g fat
> *1.0 g carbs*

In food processor, combine cream cheese, whipping cream, whole or skim milk powder and vanilla. Process until smooth. Add vanilla whey protein, coconut, SPLENDA® Granular and melted cocoa butter (melt in microwave oven 2 minutes; stir until all bits are melted). Spread in 8-inch (20 cm) square glass baking dish. Use plastic wrap over mixture to help press out. Refrigerate until firm.

HAZELNUT RAISIN MILK CHOCOLATE

Everyone in the family loved this chocolate!

$^1/_2$ cup Confectioner's Sugar (125 mL)
  Substitute, page 65
$^1/_3$ cup butter, melted (75 mL)
$^1/_4$ cup Ketogenics® Zero-Carb (50 mL)
  Pancake Syrup*
30 SPLENDA® packets
2 oz unsweetened chocolate, (60 g)
  melted
2 tbsp whipping cream (25 mL)
$^1/_4$ cup blanched hazelnuts (50 mL)
$^1/_4$ cup raisins (50 mL)

Yield: 40 (4 x 10) pieces
1 piece
38.4 calories
0.6 g protein
3.2 g fat
2.3 g carbs

In medium bowl, combine Confectioner's Sugar Substitute, page 65, butter, Ketogenics® Zero-Carb Pancake Syrup and SPLENDA®. Stir in chocolate. Stir in whipping cream. Pour into 9 x 5 x 3-inch (2 L) loaf pan. Sprinkle hazelnuts and raisins over top. Press into chocolate. Freeze.

Helpful Hint: *Another brand of pancake syrup may be used; just make sure it is a thick syrup and not a very watery kind.

LIKE REAL FUDGE

This is the closest I've come to making a confection that tastes almost exactly like fudge. No one was more surprised than me!

2 oz cocoa butter (60 g)
1 oz unsweetened chocolate (30 g)
2 tbsp coconut oil (25 mL)
$^1/_2$ cup whole milk powder, OR (125 mL)
  skim milk powder
12 SPLENDA® packets
$^1/_8$ tsp salt (0.5 mL)

Yield: 27 (3 x 9) pieces
1 piece
41.2 calories
0.7 g protein
3.8 g fat
1.4 g carbs

In double boiler, over medium heat, melt cocoa butter, chocolate and coconut oil. Stir in milk powder, SPLENDA® and salt. Pour into 9 x 5 x 3-inch (2 L) loaf pan. Freeze until hard. Keep at room temperature or in the refrigerator for longer storage. (Best results with finely ground whole milk powder)

CHOCOLATE FUDGE

There is a stronger chocolate flavor is in this fudge than in fudge on page 73.

2 oz unsweetened chocolate (60 g)
2 oz cocoa butter (60 g)
2 tbsp coconut oil (25 mL)
2 tbsp unsalted, OR salted butter (25 mL)
2 tbsp whipping cream (25 mL)
$^1/_2$ cup whole milk powder, OR (125 mL)
  skim milk powder
24 SPLENDA® packets
$^1/_2$ cup vanilla whey protein (125 mL)
$^1/_4$ cup whole milk powder (50 mL)

Yield: 36 squares
1 square
59.9 calories
1.8 g protein
5.2 g fat
2.0 g carbs

In double boiler, melt chocolate and cocoa butter over medium heat. In cereal bowl, melt coconut oil and butter in microwave oven 1 minute. Stir in cream. Stir in $^1/_2$ cup (125 mL) whole milk powder or skim milk powder and SPLENDA®.

Add sweetened milk mixture to melted chocolate mixture in double boiler; stir. Remove from heat and stir in vanilla whey protein and $^1/_4$ cup (50 mL) whole milk powder. Spread in 8-inch (20 cm) square glass baking dish. Press out evenly with back of soup spoon. Freeze. When frozen solid, store in covered container either at room temperature or in the refrigerator.

Helpful Hint: This fudge can be kept at room temperature for a few days, however, for longer storage and more of a "snap" when biting into the fudge, refrigerate in a closed container.

~~Low-Carb Dieting Tip~~
Atkins is not a fad diet nor is it a crash diet. For it to be successful, it has to become a way of life. If you fall off the wagon on vacation or for a day or two or more – get back to your chosen, healthier way of life as soon as possible.

CHOCOLATE ORANGE FUDGE

When I enjoy this fudge, I think to myself, why do I ever need to buy sugar free chocolate bars (other than the convenience factor) – this is so much nicer to me. Also see Pecan Fudge, page 77.

3 cups sugarless chocolate chips (375 mL)
  {18 oz (540 g)}
1¹/₈ cups Condensed Milk, (275 mL)
  page 68
2 tsp finely grated orange peel (10 mL)
1¹/₂ tsp Cointreau, OR orange (7 mL)
  extract to taste
1 cup chopped pecans (250 mL)

Yield: 72 pieces
1 piece
59.4 calories
0.9 g protein
4.2 g fat
1.1 g carbs

In double boiler, over medium heat, melt chocolate with Condensed milk, page 68 and orange peel. Stir occasionally. As soon as chocolate has almost melted completely, add Cointreau or orange extract. Stir continuously until chocolate is melted completely. Stir in pecans and spread evenly in 9 x 13-inch (23 x 33 cm) glass baking dish. Cover dish with plastic or foil and freeze. Later refrigerate uncovered, if desired, for a fudge-like consistency or keep frozen for a more chewy consistency.

Variation: **Plain Chocolate Fudge:** Omit orange peel and Cointreau or orange extract. (***1.0 g Carbs***)

Helpful Hints: Cointreau is a mildly bitter, brandy-based liqueur, flavored with the peel of sweet and sour oranges from Curacao and Spain.

You can "play" with this recipe and use peppermint extract or whatever flavor you desire. Another idea is to divide the chocolate mixture in half and flavor the one half with one flavoring and the other half with another. Yet another idea is to replace some of the water in the Condensed Milk, with a particular flavor of Da Vinci® Sugar Free Syrup that you think will go well and omit Cointreau. You could replace some of the sugar free chocolate with unsweetened baking chocolate (equivalent weight) or cocoa butter to make a different fudge.

~~Low-Carb Dieting Tip~~
Going to a party? Offer to bring a dessert.

ALMOND KAHLUA CHOCOLATE

Try the intense chocolate frosting or the almond milk chocolate frosting for a special occasion cake.

2 oz unsweetened baking chocolate (60 g)
$^1/_4$ cup whipping cream (50 mL)
$^1/_4$ cup almond butter, softened (50 mL)
16 SPLENDA® packets
$^1/_2$ cup SPLENDA® Granular (125 mL)
$^1/_2$ cup sour cream (125 mL)
2 tbsp Da Vinci® Sugar Free (25 mL)
  Kahuli Caffe Syrup, OR your choice
$^1/_4$ cup Confectioner's Sugar Substitute, (50 mL)
  page 65
1 oz cocoa butter (30 g)
$^1/_2$ cup raw almonds, chopped (125 mL)

Yield: 36 pieces
1 piece
52.9 calories
1.2 g protein
4.7 g fat
1.9 g carbs

In medium bowl, microwave baking chocolate about 2 minutes; stir until completely melted. Stir in whipping cream. Add almond butter; stir in well. Add SPLENDA®, SPLENDA® Granular and sour cream; stir. Add Da Vinci® Sugar Free Kahuli Caffe Syrup and Confectioner's Sugar Substitute, page 65.

In cereal bowl, melt cocoa butter in microwave oven, approximately 3 minutes. Stir into chocolate. Stir in almonds. Pour into 8-inch (20 cm) square glass baking dish. Freeze. Microwave gradually, until at the right consistency for easy removal. Freeze leftovers

Variations: **Intense Chocolate Frosting:** Use all the ingredients up to and including Da Vinci® Sugar Free Kahuli Caffe Syrup. Refrigerate until at the right consistency for spreading. This could take as little as 15 minutes. Very ample frosting for a double-layered cake or for a Bundt cake (frosted in the middle and on top). *Less frosting may be used to bring down carb count.* The rest can be refrigerated for another use or just for snacking on some other day.
Yield: $1^1/_3$ cups (325 mL), 12/16 servings, 1 serving: (*4.4 g/3.3 g Carbs*)

Almond Milk Chocolate Frosting: As for the frosting above, however, use sweetened sugar free chocolate (I used chocolate chips), only 8 SPLENDA® packets for sweetening and omit Da Vinci® Sugar Free Kahuli Caffe Syrup. The almond flavor comes through much more strongly, with just a hint of chocolate. Refrigerate for an hour or more, until the frosting is at the right consistency for spreading. *Yield:* 12/16 servings, 1 serving: (*2.4 g/1.8 g Carbs*)

Da Vinci® Alternative: Use 1 tbsp (15 mL) of liqueur such as Kahlua.

TRUFFLES

These won't last long! If desired, roll some truffles in diced almonds.

$^2/_3$ cup regular cream cheese (150 mL)
$^1/_4$ cup SPLENDA® Granular (50 mL)
$^1/_4$ cup raisins, snipped in half (50 mL)
$^1/_2$ tsp rum extract (2 mL)
$^1/_4$ cup desiccated coconut, (50 mL)
  unsweetened
2 tbsp SPLENDA® Granular (25 mL)

> **Yield:** 18 truffles
> 1 truffle
> 48.4 calories
> 1.1 g protein
> 3.7 g fat
> **2.6 g carbs**

In medium bowl, combine cream cheese, $^1/_4$ cup (50 mL) SPLENDA® Granular, raisins and rum extract. Use a wooden spoon to mash everything together. On a dinner plate, combine coconut and 2 tbsp (25 mL) SPLENDA® Granular. Form small balls out of the cream cheese mixture and roll in sweetened coconut. Place in pretty bon bon cups and refrigerate.

PECAN FUDGE

Few chocolate chips are required to make this delicious milk chocolate fudge, with similar great taste of Plain Chocolate Fudge, page 75.

$1^1/_2$ oz cocoa butter (45 g)
$1^1/_8$ cups Condensed Milk, (275 mL)
  page 68
$^1/_2$ cup chocolate chips, (125 mL)
  sugar free (sweetened)
$^1/_2$ cup chopped pecans (125 mL)

> **Yield:** 36 squares
> 1 square
> 62.4 calories
> 1.2 g protein
> 5.4 g fat
> **1.3 g carbs**

In covered cereal bowl, nuke cocoa butter about 3 minutes, or until melted. Set aside. Prepare Condensed Milk as directed on page 68. Add Condensed Milk and chocolate chips to double boiler. Stir until chocolate melts. Add pecans. Stir in cocoa butter. Pour into 8-inch (20 cm) glass baking dish. Place in freezer above refrigerator. Let thaw briefly and serve.

Helpful Hints: If you cannot tolerate maltitol in the chocolate chips, then substitute 3 oz (90 g) chocolate sweetened with another sweetener. Another option is to use 3 oz (90 g) unsweetened baking chocolate and SPLENDA® packets to taste; probably at the very least 24 packets. Da Vinci® Sugar Free Syrup may be used instead of water in Condensed Milk, page 68. (***2.1 g Carbs***)

COOKIES & SQUARES

"SUGAR" COOKIES

*These cookies are a copycat of the traditional sugar cookies. They spread nicely.
I think I prefer them to Snickerdoodles.*

1 cup butter, softened (250 mL)
3 egg yolks
2 cups SPLENDA® Granular (500 mL)
1 tsp baking soda (5 mL)
1 tsp cream of tartar (5 mL)
$^1/_2$ tsp vanilla extract (2 mL)
2 cups Low-Carb Bake Mix, (500 mL)
  page 22
$^1/_3$ cup SPLENDA® Granular (75 mL)

Yield: 60 cookies
1 cookie
50.5 calories
1.6 g protein
4.4 g fat
1.3 g carbs

In food processor with sharp blade, or in bowl with electric mixer, process butter. Add egg yolks, 2 cups (500 mL) SPLENDA® Granular, baking soda, cream of tartar and vanilla extract; process. Add Low-Carb Bake Mix, page 22; process. Place in freezer 15 minutes. Stir $^1/_3$ cup (75 mL) SPLENDA® Granular into dough. Do not worry if it does not mix in completely.

Form dough into 1-inch (2.5 cm) balls and place on ungreased cookie sheets, leaving enough room for cookies to spread slightly. Bake in 300°F (150°C) oven on upper middle shelf (i.e. one rung from top rung) 15 minutes, or until light brown underneath. Cool on cookie sheets 1 minute. Using thin, flat spatula, transfer to wire rack to further cool.

Helpful Hint: These cookies may be frosted with Lemon Cheese Frosting, page 72, if desired. That's how my son, Jonathan, likes them. Personally, I prefer them plain.

~~Low-Carb Dieting Tip~~
*Choose a realistic goal weight and aim for it. Plan each month's weight loss
goals in advance and then work towards it.*

SNICKERDOODLES

Old-fashioned cookies rolled in a sweet cinnamon mixture.

$^1/_2$ cup butter, softened (125 mL)
1 egg
1 cup SPLENDA® Granular (250 mL)
$^1/_2$ tsp vanilla extract (2 mL)
$^1/_4$ tsp baking soda (1 mL)
$^1/_4$ tsp cream of tartar (1 mL)
$1^2/_3$ cups Low-Carb Bake Mix, (400 mL)
  page 22
2 tbsp SPLENDA® Granular (25 mL)
1 tsp cinnamon (5 mL)

Yield: 36 cookies
1 cookie
51.0 calories
2.2 g protein
4.1 g fat
1.3 g carbs

In food processor with sharp blade, or in bowl using electric mixer, process butter. Add egg, 1 cup (250 mL) SPLENDA® Granular, vanilla extract, baking soda and cream of tartar; process. Add Low-Carb Bake Mix, page 22; process. Chill dough about half an hour or until dough is easy to handle.

Shape dough into 1-inch (2.5 cm) balls. In small bowl combine 2 tbsp (25 mL) SPLENDA® Granular and cinnamon. Roll balls in mixture and place on ungreased cookie sheet. Bake in 375°F (190°C) oven 10 minutes. Transfer to wire rack and allow to cool.

Helpful Hints: This recipe also works very well with $1^1/_2$ cups (375 mL) Vital Ultimate Bake Mix, page 20.

These cookies do not spread that much. I've also flattened them with a fork, however, prefer to leave them in ball shapes.

~~Low-Carb Dieting Tip~~
Have your blood work done, blood pressure and random glucose level tested, including thyroid hormone levels (if you're hypothyroid) determined, before beginning the diet and during and after. It will be very interesting to compare notes down the road.

SPICED PUMPKIN CHIP COOKIES

Pumpkin adds moistness – great Thanksgiving cookies! The frosting makes the cookies more appealing to children. Delicious!

$2^3/_4$ cups Low-Carb Bake Mix, (675 mL)
  page 22
$1^1/_4$ cups SPLENDA® Granular (300 mL)
2 tsp baking powder (10 mL)
$1^1/_2$ tsp pumpkin pie spice (7 mL)
$^1/_2$ tsp baking soda (2 mL)
$^1/_4$ tsp salt (1 mL)
1 cup butter, softened (250 mL)
10 oz cooked, mashed pumpkin (300 g)
2 eggs
1 tsp vanilla extract (5 mL)
2 cups sugar free chocolate chips (500 mL)
1 cup chopped pecans (250 mL)
Confectioner's Sugar Frosting: (optional)
1 cup Confectioner's Sugar Substitute, (250 mL)
  page 65
2 tbsp whipping cream (25 mL)
2 tbsp Da Vinci® Sugar Free Vanilla, OR (25 mL)
  Caramel Syrup, OR Low-Carb Pancake Syrup
1 tbsp butter, melted (15 mL)
$^1/_2$ cup Crème Fraiche, page 67 (125 mL)

Yield: 68 cookies
1 cookie
83.5 calories
2.3 g protein
6.5 g fat
1.7 g carbs

In large bowl, combine Low-Carb Bake Mix, page 22, SPLENDA® Granular, baking powder, pumpkin pie spice, baking soda and salt.

In food processor or in large bowl with electric mixer, process butter. Add pumpkin, eggs and vanilla extract; process. Gradually add dry ingredients and process until completely incorporated. Stir in chocolate chips and pecans. Drop by heaping $1^1/_2$ teaspoonfuls (7 mL) onto greased cookie sheets. Bake in 350°F (180°C) oven 12 to 15 minutes, or until edges are turning light brown and cookies are golden brown underneath. Remove with very thin, broad spatula (or something similar) to wire rack to cool completely.

Confectioner's Sugar Frosting: In small bowl, combine Confectioner's Sugar Substitute, page 65, whipping cream, Da Vinci® Sugar Free Syrup of choice and butter. Fold in Crème Fraiche, page 67. Cookies with frosting: (***2.3 g Carbs***)

Variation:* Spiced Pumpkin Jumble Cookies:** Omit chocolate chips. Use 2 cups (500 mL) chopped pecans and $^1/_2$ cup (125 mL) raisins, snipped in half. (2.5 g Carbs***)

CREAM CHEESE COOKIES

They taste almost like shortbread. They remain fresh a long time.

1 cup butter, softened (250 mL)
8 oz regular cream cheese, (250 g)
  softened
$1^1/_4$ cups SPLENDA® Granular (300 mL)
1 tsp vanilla extract (5 mL)
$^1/_4$ tsp salt (1 mL)
$2^3/_4$ cups Low-Carb Bake Mix, (675 mL)
  page 22
$^1/_2$ cup chopped pecans (125 mL)

> *Yield:* 108 cookies
> 1 cookie
> 39.4 calories
> 1.4 g protein
> 3.5 g fat
> *0.7 g carbs*

In food processor with sharp blade or in bowl with electric mixer, process butter and cream cheese together. Add SPLENDA® Granular, vanilla extract and salt; process. While processing, gradually add Low-Carb Bake Mix, page 22. Stir in pecans. Shape into 4 rolls, 6-inches long x 2-inches wide (15 cm x 5 cm). Refrigerate rolls in wax paper overnight.

Thinly slice each roll into 27 cookies. Place on ungreased cookie sheets and bake in 300°F (150°C) oven 15 minutes, or until slightly browned underneath. Cool on cookie sheets. Place in closed container in refrigerator, as they taste best chilled. They remain fresh a long time.

FUDGE FANTASIES

Excellent dark brown, chocolate-y cookies filled with nuts and chocolate chips!

2 cups sugarless chocolate chips (500 mL)
2 oz unsweetened chocolate (60 g)
2 tbsp butter (25 mL)
2 eggs
16 SPLENDA® packets
$^1/_3$ cup Low-Carb Bake Mix, (75 mL)
  page 22
$^1/_4$ tsp baking powder (1 mL)
1 cup chopped pecans, OR other nuts (250 mL)

> *Yield:* 40 cookies
> 1 cookie
> 79.3 calories
> 1.4 g protein
> 5.9 g fat
> *1.4 g carbs*

In double boiler, melt 1 cup (250 mL) chocolate chips, unsweetened chocolate and butter. Remove from heat. Stir in eggs, one at a time. Stir in SPLENDA®, Low-Carb Bake Mix, page 22, baking powder, remaining chocolate chips and chopped pecans or nuts of choice. Drop by $1^1/_2$ teaspoonfuls (7 mL) onto greased cookie sheets, allowing room for spreading. Bake in 350°F (180°C) oven 8 minutes, or until edges are firm and surface of cookies are no longer shiny. Transfer with flat, thin spatula to wire rack to cool.

CLASSIC PEANUT BUTTER COOKIES
A traditional peanut butter cookie recipe gone low-carb.

$^1/_2$ cup butter, softened (125 mL)
$^1/_2$ cup peanut butter, without (125 mL)
  sugar or salt
1 cup SPLENDA® Granular, (250 mL)
  OR 24 SPLENDA® packets
1 tsp molasses (5 mL)
1 tsp vanilla extract (5 mL)
$^1/_2$ tsp baking soda (2 mL)
$^1/_2$ tsp baking powder (2 mL)
$^1/_8$ tsp salt (0.5 mL)
1 egg
$1^1/_2$ cups Low-Carb Bake Mix, (375 mL)
  page 22

Yield: 36 cookies
1 cookie
69.4 calories
2.8 g protein
5.7 g fat
1.7 g carbs

In food processor with sharp blade or in bowl with electric mixer, process butter and peanut butter until smooth. Add SPLENDA® Granular, molasses, vanilla extract, baking soda, baking powder and salt; process. Add egg; process. Add Low-Carb Bake Mix, page 22; process until combined. Refrigerate until easy to handle.

Form 1-inch (2.5 cm) balls. Roll in additional SPLENDA® Granular, if desired, and place on ungreased cookie sheet. Leave about an inch (2.5 cm) of space between cookies. Flatten cookies with fork in crisscross fashion. Bake in 375°F (190°C) oven 7 minutes, or until bottoms are lightly browned.

Variations: **Chocolate Peanut Butter Cookies:** Drizzle cookies with Drizzling Chocolate, page 171, *Splendid Low-Carbing* (***2.1 g Carbs***), or melt sugarless chocolate chips or a low-carb chocolate bar with a little butter and use that to drizzle over cookies to add interest and extra flavor.

Almond Butter Cookies: Substitute almond butter and add $^1/_2$ tsp (2 mL) almond extract in addition to vanilla extract. (***1.9 g Carbs***)

~~Low-Carb Dieting Tip~~
Many prescription medications slow or inhibit weight loss or even contribute to weight gain. Do not take any unnecessary medications.

LEMON CURD TARTLETS

Very lemony tartlets with a little Crème Fraiche to moderate that.

Pastry:
1 cup Vital Oat Ultimate (250 mL)
  Bake Mix, page 20
4 oz regular cream cheese, (125 g)
  softened
2 tbsp butter (25 mL)
2 tbsp almond butter (25 mL)
2 SPLENDA® packets
$1/4$ tsp almond extract (1 mL)

Filling:
1 recipe Lemon Curd, page 60,
  Splendid Low-Carbing for Life, Vol. 1
1 tsp Crème Fraiche, page 67 (5 mL)
  per tartlet

Yield: 20 tartlets
1 tartlet
107.7 calories
3.0 g protein
9.5 g fat
2.8 g carbs

Pastry: In food processor with sharp blade or in bowl with electric mixer, process Vital Oat Ultimate Bake Mix, page 20, cream cheese, butter, almond butter, SPLENDA® and almond extract. Form into a ball.

Break off 20 balls, each weighing 0.5 oz (15 g). Press balls into mini muffin cups and up sides. Bake in 350°F (180°C) oven 10 minutes.

Filling: Prepare Lemon Curd, page 60, *Splendid Low-Carbing for Life*, Vol. 1. Fill pastry shells with chilled Lemon Curd and Crème Fraiche, page 67 on top. Refrigerate until serving time.

Helpful Hint: If desired, refrigerate dough until easier to use.

~~Low-Carb Dieting Tip~~
When first beginning a low-carb diet, fatigue, headaches and crankiness are common. It takes a few days for the body to adjust and switch from a glucose burning metabolism to primarily a fat burning metabolism (your fat!).

COCONUT SULTANA COOKIES

Delectable cookies! These did not last the day with our family.

$^2/_3$ cup finely grated coconut, (150 mL)
 (unsweetened)
2 tbsp SPLENDA® Granular (25 mL)
$^1/_2$ cup butter, softened (125 mL)
2 tsp finely grated lemon peel (10 mL)
1 egg
1 cup SPLENDA® Granular (250 mL)
$1^1/_2$ cups Low-Carb Bake Mix, (375 mL)
 page 22
$^1/_4$ tsp baking soda (1 mL)
$^1/_8$ tsp salt (0.5 mL)
$^1/_2$ cup sour cream (125 mL)
$^1/_2$ cup sultanas, OR seedless raisins (125 mL)

Yield: 48 cookies
1 cookie
54.4 calories
1.7 g protein
4.2 g fat
2.4 g carbs

Combine coconut and 2 tbsp (25 mL) SPLENDA® Granular and spread out on dinner plate. Set aside.

In food processor or in bowl with electric mixer, process butter and lemon peel. Add egg and 1 cup (250 mL) SPLENDA® Granular; process.

In medium bowl, combine Low-Carb Bake Mix, page 22, baking soda and salt. Add to food processor alternately with sour cream. Mix in sultanas or raisins. Leave mixture on counter top 20 minutes.

Roll teaspoons of cookie batter into balls and roll in sweetened coconut. Place on lightly greased cookie sheets, leaving spaces between cookies for slight spreading. Bake in 350°F (180°C) oven 10 to 12 minutes, or until golden brown underneath. Cool on cookie sheets.

~~Low-Carb Dieting Tip~~
A half-hearted attempt at low-carbing will make you feel better, but will probably not result in much weight loss.

THE BEST BROWNIES

If your system can tolerate maltitol in the sugarless chocolate chips, these brownies will delight you. Do be warned that they are very addictive. For those who can't tolerate sugar alcohols, see delicious brownies on page 88.

8 oz sugarless chocolate chips, (250 g)
  (sweetened) - about $1^1/_3$ cups (325 mL)
1 cup regular butter (salted) (250 mL)
4 eggs
2 cups SPLENDA® Granular (500 mL)
2 tsp vanilla extract (10 mL)
$^1/_8$ tsp salt (0.5 mL)
1 cup Vital Ultimate Bake Mix, (250 mL)
  page 20 (using spelt flour)

Frosting:
$^1/_2$ cup sugarless chocolate chips (125 mL)
2 tbsp butter (25 mL)
1 SPLENDA® packet (optional)

Yield: 36 brownies
1 brownie
120.9 calories
2.0 g protein
9.2 g fat
2.8 g carbs

In double boiler, melt chocolate chips and butter. Stir until smooth.

In large bowl, whisk eggs with wire whisk. Whisk in SPLENDA® Granular, vanilla extract and salt. Add chocolate mixture; whisk in. Fold in Vital Ultimate Bake Mix, page 20.

Pour into lightly greased 9 x 13-inch (23 x 33 cm) glass baking dish. Bake in 350°F (180°C) oven 25 minutes, or until cake tester comes out clean. Spread frosting over warm cake. Cool in pan on wire rack. Cut into squares, cover and refrigerate. These are best several hours later or preferably the next day, if you can wait that long!

Frosting: In double boiler, melt chocolate chips and butter. Stir in SPLENDA®, if using.

Helpful Hints: I've made these brownies with salted butter and $^1/_4$ tsp (1 mL) salt and my husband loved them. I thought they needed just a little less salt, but you will probably make these on more than one occasion, so you be the judge and see which version you prefer. Warm, these are fluffy in texture, at room temperature after a few hours they're slightly denser, but after several hours of refrigeration, they become deliciously dense.

ECSTASY SQUARES

The crust for these squares tastes similar to a graham cracker crust. These squares have a different name, actually. Maybe you can remember?

Graham Cracker-Like Crust:
1 cup Low-Carb Bake Mix, (250 mL)
  page 22
1 cup ground almonds (250 mL)
$^1/_2$ cup butter, melted (125 mL)
2 SPLENDA® packets
Filling:
8 oz regular cream cheese, (250 g)
  softened
1 cup Crème Fraiche, page 67 (250 mL)
$^1/_4$ cup Da Vinci® Sugar Free (50 mL)
  French Vanilla Syrup, OR Zero Carb Pancake Syrup
1 tbsp whipping cream (15 mL)
8 SPLENDA® packets
1 tsp vanilla extract (5 mL)
Topping:
2 packages instant diet chocolate pudding, OR
  (one chocolate and one vanilla diet pudding)
1 cup whipping cream (250 mL)
1 cup water (250 mL)

Yield: 40 squares
1 square
99.7 calories
2.4 g protein
9.0 g fat
2.5 g carbs

Graham Cracker-like Crust: In medium bowl, combine Low-Carb Bake Mix, page 22, ground almonds, butter and SPLENDA®. Press in bottom of 9 x 13-inch (23 x 33 cm) glass baking dish. Bake in 350°F (180°C) oven 12 minutes, or until light golden brown.

Filling: In food processor with sharp blade, blender or in bowl with electric mixer, process cream cheese until smooth. Add Crème Fraiche, page 67, Da Vinci® Sugar Free French Vanilla Syrup, whipping cream, SPLENDA® and vanilla extract. Drop blobs over cooled crust and spread very gently and carefully.

Topping: In food processor, or in bowl with electric mixer, process puddings, whipping cream and water on lowest speed until thickened.

Spread pudding mixture over cream cheese layer with flat surface of dinner knife. Chill.

CREAM CHEESE CAKE BARS

This recipe is from Angie Berglund. Her husband liked the high carb version so much, that he requested it for Christmas. This low-carb version is for Angie.

8 oz light cream cheese (250 g)
4 oz butter, softened (125 g)
$^1/_4$ cup whipping cream (50 mL)
2 eggs
$1^1/_2$ cups SPLENDA® Granular (375 mL)
1 tsp vanilla extract (5 mL)
$2^1/_4$ cups Vital Oat Ultimate (550 mL)
  Bake Mix, page 20
$2^1/_2$ tsp baking powder (12 mL)
$^1/_2$ tsp baking soda (2 mL)
$^1/_4$ tsp salt (1 mL)
1 cup sugarless chocolate chips, (250 mL)
  (sweetened)

Yield: 36 bars
1 bar
108.9 calories
3.1 g protein
8.2 g fat
3.1 g carbs

In food processor or in bowl with electric mixer, process cream cheese until smooth. Add butter; process. Add whipping cream, eggs, SPLENDA® Granular and vanilla extract; process.

In large bowl, combine Vital Oat Ultimate Bake Mix, page 20, baking powder, baking soda and salt. Add cream cheese mixture and stir just until moistened. Stir in chocolate chips. Fill two greased 9 x 5 x 3-inch (2 L) loaf pans. Bake in 350°F (180°C) oven 40 to 50 minutes, or until cake tester comes out clean.

Allow to cool on wire rack. Remove loaves and cut each loaf into 9 thick slices and cut down the center of each slice to make 18 bars per loaf.

Helpful Hints: These fudgy cake loaves are not meant to rise very much – just high enough to make substantial bars. These bars are deliciously moist the first day, however, they do not last well past the third day. They have a better texture at room temperature than when chilled.

~~Low-Carb Dieting Tip~~
Dr. Atkins, a cardiologist, was convinced that his diet is heart-healthy and that it should be the diet of choice for folks struggling with obesity and/or diabetes. Many enlightened, mainstream doctors today will concur. Before beginning the diet, read his book and consult a doctor.

FROSTED FUDGE BROWNIES

Fabulous dark chocolate, melt-in-your-mouth brownies with a rich frosting.

1 $^1/_2$ cups SPLENDA® Granular (375 mL)
$^2/_3$ cup Crème Fraiche, page 67 (150 mL)
$^1/_4$ cup whole or skim milk (50 mL)
  powder
2 oz baking chocolate, (60 g)
  (unsweetened)
2 tbsp butter, softened (25 mL)
1 tsp vanilla extract (5 mL)
2 eggs
$^2/_3$ cup Low-Carb Bake Mix, page 22 (150 mL)
Chocolate Fudge Frosting:
$^1/_3$ cup Crème Fraiche, page 67 (75 mL)
5 SPLENDA® packets, OR to taste
2 tbsp whole or skim milk powder* (25 mL)
1 oz unsweetened baking chocolate (30 g)

Yield: 25 brownies
1 brownie
75.4 calories
2.5 g protein
6.0 g fat
3.3 g carbs

In medium bowl, combine SPLENDA® Granular, Crème Fraiche, page 67 and whole or skim milk powder. In cereal bowl, microwave baking chocolate 2 minutes; stir until completely melted. Stir into Crème Fraiche mixture until well combined. Place chocolate mixture in food processor with sharp blade, blender or in bowl with electric mixer. Add butter, vanilla extract and eggs; process until smooth. Add Low-Carb Bake Mix, page 22; process. Spread evenly in 8-inch (20 cm) glass baking dish sprayed with nonstick cooking spray.

Bake in 350°F (180°C) oven 15 minutes, or until cake tester comes out clean. Spread frosting over warm brownies. Cool in pan on wire rack. Cut into squares when cool. Best served at room temperature.

Chocolate Fudge Frosting: In small bowl, combine Crème Fraiche, page 67, SPLENDA® and whole milk powder. Stir well. In cereal bowl, microwave chocolate 2 minutes to melt; stir to melt completely. Stir into Crème Fraiche mixture until well combined.

Variations: Walnut Fudge Brownies: Add $^2/_3$ cup (150 mL) chopped walnuts. (***3.5 g Carbs***)

Chocolate Chip Fudge Brownies: Add $^2/_3$ cup (150 mL) sugarless chocolate chips. (***3.5 g Carbs***)

LEMON SUPREME SQUARES

These lasted a few hours. Everyone loved them.

Base:
2 cups Low-Carb Bake Mix, (500 mL)
  page 22
$^1/_2$ cup SPLENDA® Granular (125 mL)
$^3/_4$ cup butter, melted (175 mL)
Topping:
5 eggs
$^1/_2$ cup fresh lemon juice (125 mL)
$1^1/_4$ cups SPLENDA® Granular (300 mL)
1 tbsp lemon peel (15 mL)

Yield: 36 squares
1 square
77.3 calories
3.3 g protein
6.3 g fat
2.1 g carbs

Base: In medium bowl, combine Low-Carb Bake Mix, page 22 and SPLENDA® Granular. Stir in butter. Press into 9 x 13-inch (23 x 33 cm) glass baking dish. Bake in 350°F (180°C) oven 15 minutes, or until slightly brown.

Topping: In another medium bowl, beat eggs with fork. Stir in lemon juice, SPLENDA® Granular and lemon peel. Pour over baked crust and bake in 350°F (180°C) oven 15 minutes. Refrigerate for crust to set up nicely.

CHEWY COCONUT SQUARES

Just enough raisins to produce sweet, chewy squares.

2 eggs
$^1/_2$ cup butter, melted (125 mL)
1 tsp vanilla extract (5 mL)
$^1/_4$ tsp maple extract (1 mL)
1 cup desiccated coconut, (250 mL)
  (unsweetened)
1 cup SPLENDA® Granular (250 mL)
$^1/_2$ cup Low-Carb Bake Mix, (125 mL)
  page 22
$^1/_4$ cup snipped raisins, snipped in half (50 mL)
$^1/_4$ cup chopped pecans or walnuts (50 mL)
$^1/_2$ tsp baking powder (2 mL)
$^1/_8$ tsp salt (0.5 mL)

Yield: 25 squares
1 square
90.9 calories
1.8 g protein
7.8 g fat
2.8 g carbs

In small bowl, beat eggs. Stir in slightly cooled butter, vanilla and maple extracts. In larger bowl, combine coconut, SPLENDA® Granular, Low-Carb Bake Mix, page 22, raisins, chopped pecans or walnuts, baking powder and salt. Spread evenly in 8-inch (20 cm) square glass baking dish. Bake in 350°F (180°C) oven 20 minutes.

BUTTER TART SQUARES

These old fashioned squares are sure to please.

Base:
1 cup Low-Carb Bake Mix, (250 mL)
  page 22
2 tbsp SPLENDA® Granular (25 mL)
7 tbsp butter, melted (105 mL)
Filling:
1 1/2 cups SPLENDA® Granular (375 mL)
2/3 cup chopped pecans, OR (150 mL)
  walnuts
1/3 cup raisins (75 mL)
2 tbsp vital wheat gluten (25 mL)
1/2 tsp baking powder (2 mL)
3 extra-large eggs
1 tbsp butter, melted (15 mL)
1 1/2 tsp molasses (7 mL)
1 tsp vanilla extract (5 mL)

Yield: 25 squares
1 square
96.3 calories
3.3 g protein
7.4 g fat
4.3 g carbs.

Base: In small bowl, combine Low-Carb Bake Mix, page 22 and SPLENDA® Granular. Stir in butter. Press into 8-inch (20 cm) square glass baking dish. Bake in 350°F (180°C) oven 5 minutes.

Filling: In medium bowl, combine SPLENDA® Granular, pecans or walnuts, raisins (snip half the amount of raisins in half with kitchen scissors), vital wheat gluten and baking powder. In small bowl, beat eggs with fork and stir in butter, molasses and vanilla extract. Add to dry ingredients and stir well. Pour over crust and bake in 350°F (180°C) oven 15 minutes, or until filling has set. Chill.

~~Low-Carb Dieting Tip~~
Do not overlook the benefits of stretching as a form of exercise. This prevents stiffness and inflexibility of the spine and joints as we age. Personally, I enjoy ballet video tapes and exercise frequently using those.

GLAZED LEMON RASPBERRY BARS
Tart lemon bars with a hint of raspberry – pretty bars!

Base:
2 cups Low-Carb Bake Mix, (500 mL)
 page 22
$^1/_4$ cup SPLENDA® Granular (50 mL)
$^3/_4$ cup butter, PLUS 2 tbsp, (200 mL)
 melted

Topping:
$^1/_2$ cup raspberry fruit spread, (125 mL)
 sugar free (sieved to remove seeds)
4 extra-large eggs
$1^1/_2$ cup SPLENDA® Granular (375 mL)
2 tbsp vital wheat gluten (25 mL)
$^1/_2$ tsp baking powder (2 mL)
$^1/_2$ cup lemon juice (125 mL)
3 tbsp water (45 mL)

Glaze:
$^1/_2$ cup Confectioner's Sugar Substitute, (125 mL)
 page 65
2 tbsp butter, melted (25 mL)
1 tbsp lemon juice (15 mL)
2 tbsp water (25 mL)

Yield: 42 (7 x 6) bars
1 bar
82.2 caloires
3.3 g protein
6.5 g fat
2.8 g carbs

Base: In medium bowl, combine Low-Carb Bake Mix, page 22, SPLENDA® Granular and butter. Place in 9 x 13-inch (23 x 33 cm) glass baking dish. Cover with plastic wrap; press crust out. Bake in 350°F (180°C) oven 10 minutes. Cool.

Topping: In small nonstick saucepan, heat raspberry fruit spread. Drizzle over warm crust and spread gently with back of dessertspoon to cover crust. In food processor, in blender or in bowl with electric mixer, process eggs. Add SPLENDA® Granular, vital wheat gluten and baking powder; process, scraping sides occasionally. Add lemon juice and water; process. Pour over raspberry layer. Bake in 350°F (180°C) oven 15 minutes, or until set. When cooled, spread glaze gently over top. Refrigerate and when chilled cut into bars.

Glaze: In cereal bowl, combine Confectioner's Sugar Substitute, page 65, butter, lemon juice and water. If necessary, add a little extra water, a teaspoon at a time.

INDEX

A

B

C

Splendid Low-Carb Desserts

VANILLA ICE CREAM 31
VANILLA PEACH JELLY 27
FRUITY ICE CREAMS 31
FUDGE FANTASIES 81

M

MANDARIN ORANGE JELLY 27
MANDARIN ORANGE PEACH JELLY 27
MASCARPONE SUBSTITUTE 24
MINI SOUR CREAM POUND CAKES 44
MINT TRUFFLE COCOA 8
MOLASSES SUBSTITUTE 71

G

GINGERBREAD 51
GLAZED BLUEBERRY CHEESE PIE 34
GLAZED LEMON RASPBERRY BARS 91
GLAZED RASPBERRY CHEESE PIE 34
GLAZED STRAWBERRY CHEESE PIE 34
GOLDEN FRUITCAKE 48
GRAHAM CRACKER-LIKE CRUST 41 & 86

N

NEW YORK CHEESECAKE 58
NUT-FREE OAT ULTIMATE BAKE MIX 21
NUT-FREE ULTIMATE BAKE MIX 21

H

HAZELNUT RAISIN MILK CHOCOLATE 73
HOT CHOCOLATE DRINK MIX 9

O

ORANGE CHEESE FROSTING 72
ORANGE CHEESECAKE 54
ORANGE CREAMSICLES 26

I

ICED CAFFE LATTE 10
ICING 48
INSTANT CARAMEL SAUCE 69
INSTANT FRUITY ICE CREAM 29
INSTANT STRAWBERRY FROZ. YOGURT 28
INTENSE CHOCOLATE FROSTING 76

P

PEACH ICE CREAM 29
PEACH YOGURT SHAKE 11
PEACHES AND CREAM CHEESECAKE 53
PEACHES AND CREAM TRIFLE 24
PEANUT BUTTER CHIP PIE 38
PEANUT BUTTER CHOC. CHEESECAKE 56
PECAN CHOCOLATE SWEETHEART CAKE 50
PECAN FUDGE 77

K

KAHLUA HOT COCOA 8
KEY LIME PIE 36

PIES

ALMOND BUTTER CHIP PIE 38
ALMOND CHOCOLATE CRUST 38
ALMOND CRUST 40
BUTTERSCOTCH CREAM PIE 40
CHOCOLATE CREAM PIE 40
CHOCOLATE MINT ICE CREAM PIE 41
CHOCOLATE PECAN PIE 35
FRENCH SILK PIE 70
GLAZED BLUEBERRY CHEESE PIE 34
GLAZED RASPBERRY CHEESE PIE 34
GLAZED STRAWBERRY CHEESE PIE 34
GRAHAM CRACKER-LIKE CRUST 41 & 86
KEY LIME PIE 36
LEMON CREAM PIE 40
PEANUT BUTTER CHIP PIE 38
REFRIGERATOR PIECRUSTS 43
SINGLE PIECRUST 42
SNOW-CAPPED PUMPKIN PIE 32
STRAWBERRY CREAM PIE 39
STRAWBERRY FROZ. ICE CREAM PIE 37
STRAWBERRY RASPB. CRUMBLE TART 33

L

LEMON CHEESE FROSTING 72
LEMON CHEESECAKE 54
LEMON CREAM PIE 40
LEMON CURD TARTLETS 83
LEMON SUPREME SQUARES 89
LEMON TEA CAKE 47
LEMONY DELIGHT MUFFINS 13
LEMONY GLAZE 13
LIKE REAL FUDGE 73
LIME CHEESECAKE 54
LOW-CARB BAKE MIX 22

Splendid Low-Carb Desserts

STRAWBERRY RHUBARB CRUMBLE TART 33
VANILLA CREAM PIE 40
PLAIN CHOCOLATE FUDGE 75
PUMPKIN CHIP MUFFINS 12
PUMPKIN PECAN MUFFINS 12
PUMPKIN PECAN CHIP MUFFINS 12

R

RASPBERRY CHEESECAKE 55
RASPBERRY JELLY 27
RASPBERRY LEMON CHEESECAKE 63
RASPBERRY PINEAPPLE CREAMSICLES 26
RASPBERRY TOPPING 63
REFRIGERATOR PIECRUSTS 43
RICH MAN'S CARAMEL CUSTARD 30

S

SHORT CRUST 54
SINGLE PIECRUST 42
SNICKERDOODLES 79
SNOW PUDDING 28
SNOW-CAPPED PUMPKIN PIE 32
SPICED PEAR YOGURT SHAKE 11
SPICED PUMPKIN CHIP COOKIES 80
SPICED PUMPKIN JUMBLE COOKIES 80
SPICY CHIFFON CAKE 52
STICKY CHOCOLATE TOFFEE 65
STICKY COCONUT MILK CHOC. TOFFEE 65
STICKY VANILLA CARAMEL TOFFEE 65
STRAWBERRY BANANA SMOOTHIE 11
STRAWBERRY CHEESECAKE 55
STRAWBERRY CREAM PIE 39
STRAWBERRY FROZ. ICE CREAM PIE 37
STRAWBERRY ICE CREAM 29
STRAWBERRY JELLY 27

STRAWBERRY ORANGE CREAMSICLES 26
STRAWBERRY RASPBERRY CRUMBLE TART 33
STRAWBERRY RHUBARB CRUMBLE TART 33
STRAWBERRY SAUCE 55
"SUGAR" COOKIES 78

T

THE BEST BROWNIES 85
THICKENING AGENT 66
TOASTED COCONUT ICE CREAM 31
TOASTED COCONUT LOAF 16
TRUFFLES 77

V

VANILLA CHEESECAKE 59
VANILLA COCONUT TOFFEE 72
VANILLA CREAM PIE 40
VANILLA ICE CREAM 31
VANILLA PEACH JELLY 27
VANILLA WHEY FROSTING 64
VITAL OAT ULTIMATE BAKE MIX 20
VITAL ULTIMATE BAKE MIX 20
VITAL WHOLE WHEAT ULT. BAKE MIX 20

W

WALNUT FUDGE BROWNIES 88
WHITE CHOCOLATE FROSTING 71
WHITE CHOCOLATE SAUCE 71
WHITE HOT CHOCOLATE 10

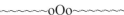

ORDERING INFORMATION

(All Prices below include S&H via USPS media mail)

SPLENDID LOW-CARBING $24 US

MORE SPLENDID LOW-CARBING $17 US

SPLENDID LOW-CARBING FOR LIFE (Volume-1) $17 US

SPLENDID LOW-CARB DESSERTS $17 US

Order <u>all 4</u> **"SPLENDID LOW-CARBING" cookbooks** $65 US

Also, you can still order **SPLENDID DESSERTS** $13 US

And **MORE SPLENDID DESSERTS** $15 US

Or order <u>Both of these</u> **"SPLENDID DESSERTS" cookbooks** $26 US

Any/All of these books can be ordered by MAIL simply by
sending your selections and a check, money order or bank draft to:

**Aurum Group
PO Box 907,
Great Falls, MT
USA 59403**
BUT, *please allow 4-8 weeks for delivery when ordering by mail!*

Or *save money* and get these books much sooner by ordering SECURELY online from:
www.sweety.com or www.Low-Carb.us Also *look for these books to be available through **Amazon.com**'s very popular website by searching AMAZON using "ALL PRODUCTS" and look for "Jennifer Eloff" and then scroll down to the zSHOPS listing at the bottom where these books will be listed in Jennifer's low-carb bookstore, or go to:* www.Sweety.com/Amazon.php for the relevant links to the **Amazon.com** listings for these books.

Please note: Recipes in *Splendid Desserts* and *More Splendid Desserts* can be adapted to suit a low-carb lifestyle by using your choice of the "Ultimate Bake Mixes" in the low-carb books. Inquiries can be sent to the above address or emailed **Desserts@Sweety.com**